RECONNECT

"What I love most about this book is that Ed Cyzewski is not presenting us with a litany of information and then requiring us to ditch our
cell phones at the side of the road and leave our technological society
behind. What he's asking us to do is open our eyes. Open our eyes
to what social media is doing to our young people. Open our eyes to
what screens are doing to us. And remember—remember that true
discipleship, true relationship, and true spiritual formation are found
in the quiet places, the still places, the merciful places."

—**SHAWN SMUCKER**, author of *Once We Were Strangers*

"I am among the blip-sized generation who eagerly anticipated being
assigned an email address ending in .edu—the key to the magical
world of Facebook in the early 2000s. Social media has been a continual source of entertainment and education for me, and it wasn't until
2016 that I began to question the amount of time I was spending on
these sites—let alone why I was spending so much time on them. Ed
Cyzewski (whom, ironically, I met through Facebook) has been an in-
valuably wise guide as I've started down the path of being intentional
in my engagement with social media. *Reconnect* is a deeply practical,
beautifully written invitation to consider anew how best to cultivate a
life of connection to God and neighbor."

—**MEGAN WESTRA**, pastor and author of *Born Again and Again*

"Ed Cyzewski winsomely demonstrates how our uncritical use and
overuse of digital media malforms us. In his beautiful description,
it 'blinds us to the brilliance of God.' I, for one, don't want to blind
myself to God's brilliance, to God's life. Here, Cyzewski is the best
kind of guide; he practices what he preaches. What's more, he doesn't
leave us stranded by merely pointing out the wrong. He leads the
way by practically showing us how to make things right with God,
ourselves, and the world. This is all serious business—and this book
is sorely needed in this moment—for the sake of our individual and
collective soul!"

—**MARLENA GRAVES**, author of *The Way Up Is Down*

"As an author and public speaker, I am constantly wondering how to engage with social media and the people around me in a healthier way. Ed Cyzewski's book, which so wonderfully displays the kindness that he embodies every day, offers us an invitation to lean into our technological world while staying tethered to discipline and simplicity through soul work and contemplative spirituality. If you desire to engage with the world but don't want to be constantly distracted by it, this is a beautiful book with important insights for all of us."

—**KAITLIN CURTICE**, author of *Glory Happening*

"Ed Cyzewski is a deep soul, making sense of living in the modern world. In this book, he takes on the digital tsunami that has swamped our lives and the spiritual damage it creates. Thankfully, Ed guides us in the way out. He shows us how to remain rooted in what matters most, even when we must be clicking and swiping. His distinction between digital and spiritual formation alone is a game changer. Highly recommended."

—**BRADLEY WRIGHT**, professor of sociology at the University of Connecticut

RECONNECT

Spiritual Restoration *from* Digital Distraction

ED CYZEWSKI

HERALD
PRESS

Harrisonburg, Virginia

Herald Press
PO Box 866, Harrisonburg, Virginia 22803
www.HeraldPress.com

Library of Congress Cataloging-in-Publication Data
Names: Cyzewski, Ed, 1979- author.
Title: Reconnect : spiritual restoration from digital distraction / Ed Cyzewski.
Description: Harrisonburg, Virginia : Herald Press, 2020. | Includes
  bibliographical references.
Identifiers: LCCN 2019040482 (print) | LCCN 2019040483 (ebook) | ISBN
  9781513806358 (paperback) | ISBN 9781513806365 (hardcover) | ISBN
  9781513806372 (ebook)
Subjects: LCSH: Spirituality—Christianity. | Spiritual life—Christianity.
  | Technology—Religious aspects—Christianity. | Social media—Religious
  aspects—Christianity.
Classification: LCC BV4501.3 .C995 2020 (print) | LCC BV4501.3 (ebook)
  | DDC 261.5/2--dc23
LC record available at https://lccn.loc.gov/2019040482
LC ebook record available at https://lccn.loc.gov/2019040483

RECONNECT
© 2020 by Herald Press, Harrisonburg, Virginia 22803. 800-245-7894.
  All rights reserved.
Library of Congress Control Number: 2019040482
International Standard Book Number: 978-1-5138-0635-8 (paperback);
978-1-5138-0636-5 (hardcover); 978-1-5138-0637-2 (ebook)
Printed in United States of America
Cover and interior design by Merrill Miller
Cover image adapted from Scully/Getty Images

Unless otherwise noted, Scripture text is quoted, with permission, from the
New Revised Standard Version, © 1989, Division of Christian Education of
the National Council of Churches of Christ in the United States of America.

24 23 22 21 20   10 9 8 7 6 5 4 3 2 1

CONTENTS

FOREWORD

In September of 2013, I walked away from the bottle. It'd been a long season of over-imbibing, of drowning the acute pain of a sick child in too much gin. But in a Methodist church lobby in Austin, Texas, the Epiphany found me, shook me awake, and told me it was time to face the world undrunk. And face the world undrunk I did, at least for a season.

Weeks passed. Then a month. Then another. A year was in the rearview mirror, and the scent of juniper berries and quinine was little more than a faint memory wafting across my hippocampus. It was the anniversary of my liquor-free life. Congratulations to me. Right?

In that long stretch of those teetotaling months, a sort of pride set in. I wasn't drinking to dull the pain anymore, and I'd rediscovered the divine love that reordered my thirsts. But did that mean I was full-on sober? If I was, how come I seemed to turn to the unholy trinity of distraction—Facebook, Twitter, Netflix—at the end of any anxious day? Why was I so often distracted from the voice of God in the real world around me?

Was it possible that I was digitally drunk? Yes, indeed.

Is it possible I still am? Perhaps, but don't tell my priest.

We live in the age of technological heroin, a day where the pushers in Silicon Valley have created digital drugs as potent as any narcotic. Social media—its equal parts feast, famine, fear, ego, and spectacular debacle. The content (at least the non-advertisement content) and means of delivery are designed to chemically hook our brains. You know this to be true. Don't you? No matter how much you swear off it, don't you always end up back on the social media sauce? I do. Why? Because the tech giants know their craft. They know how one notification grabs attention, how it hooks us, how it sets the brain on fire, how it makes a simple promise: *This tweet, this post, this "like" brings the fix.*

I've given into this fix over the years, and if there's anything I can say with some certainty, it's this: There have been seasons where I've been spiritually formed more by social media than by the Spirit of divine love. Drunk on social media, I've fallen headlong into worthless arguments, idiotic debates, and scorching political dumpster fires. I've been blocked by a Christian money guru who reckoned me a troll (rightly, perhaps) because I called him a prosperity theologian. (Dave, if you're reading this, I'm sorry.) I've spent countless hours *scrolling the feed* when I could have been sitting in silence and solitude. I've given countless hours to a medium that can't give me the thing I need most: connection with divine love.

In *Reconnect*, Ed Cyzewski offers the tool I've needed for years. In these pages, he does more than rail against social media and digital manipulation (though he does his fair share of gentle railing). He offers more than the proof that we've been hijacked by a band of psycho-savvy tech wizards (though he does that, too). Here, Ed offers a well-formed Mertonian argument; namely, the digital distractions of our modern age often operate as noisy distractions from divine love. And once that barrier is exposed, he shares the deepest truth: "The goal of spiritual formation is to remove these barriers that obscure and restrain the present life of God in us."

Reconnect is a book I could have used in my early days of "sobriety." It might have shown me that laying off the sauce is not the same as true inner sobriety. It might have shown me my need for more holistic healing.

As you read this book, ask yourself whether you're a digital addict. Ask yourself whether your brain has been hijacked by the whizz kids out west. Ask yourself whether you've allowed the digital life to form you more than the divine love. If you have, turn tail and follow Ed back to the formation that comes with a more analog life. Learn to reconnect with the physical world around you. You won't be sorry.

—Seth Haines, author of *The Book of Waking Up and Coming Clean: A Story of Faith*

A MANTRA TO RECONNECT:

Protect your time.
Prioritize one-on-one interactions.
Restore your spirit with daily silence.

Here is an unspeakable secret: paradise is all around us and we do not understand. It is wide open. The sword is taken away, but we do not know it: we are off "one to his farm and another to his merchandise." Lights on. Clocks ticking. Thermostats working. Stoves cooking. Electric shavers filling radios with static. "Wisdom," cries the dawn deacon, but we do not attend.

—THOMAS MERTON

Introduction

I am not a monk, but I try to learn from them. Some days I compare myself to a particular monk, one I saw in a documentary a few years ago. It usually doesn't go very well.

The documentary *In Pursuit of Silence* shows a monk standing on the edge of a field, solid and unmoving, his feet planted on the ground. He barely shifts his gaze as he looks out over the field, where a solitary tree keeps a lonely watch. His hands are loosely clasped behind his back; his movements are slow, deliberate, and at peace. He has nowhere to be, nothing to accomplish. In the cut used for the documentary's trailer, he appears to have nothing useful to do.

In fact, the monk's utter and complete "uselessness" is about all I can see—and that's not a slight. According to Brother Paul Quenon of the Abbey of Gethsemani, the monastic life is a "useless life."[1] This monk standing in the field is jarring in his unhurried simplicity. He appears fully committed to, well, standing around. He reminds me that some people have made the space to accept being present in the moment—full stop.

My family and I live near a field that's a bit like that monk's field. It's bordered by roads that roar with cars, trucks, and the occasional motorcycle, but it's quiet enough, still enough, and earthy enough to provide a measure of solitude. I try to find time for this field several times each week. More often than not, I walk the path through an arboretum that adjoins the field.

Yet as much as I try to be like that monk while I'm there—to find a measure of peace and silence and even uselessness—there remains a utility, pace, and purposefulness to my walking. There's no standing still, no drinking in my surroundings, and certainly no uselessness. My time in the field has a point. I have goals. I am trying to let go of thoughts, to beat back anxiety, to recover from draining days of parenting, to silence my soul, to reach out for God, to exercise. I'm trying to reconnect with whatever I've lost in the rush of each day in the crush of information that streams through my computer and smartphone. My time in the field feels a lot more like emergency triage than like a monk's pleasant, joyful reverie with the beauty of his surroundings.

What keeps me from enjoying the silence of a field?

Why does standing still like that monk seem impossible?

Are uselessness and presence and solitude things we have lost? Should we try to regain them?

We live immersed in distraction, stimulation, and affirmation in part because we are plugged in to technology. We never have to be alone with our thoughts. We never have to stand still without something to hold and fiddle with. We can access unlimited information on the Internet and continual interaction on social media. Our phones give us constant access to this flood of information and socialization.

Our high-tech, plugged-in, social media world appeals to us because its many conveniences, social connections, and efficiencies appear more important than its dark side of compulsive usage and exacerbation of a range of mental health challenges, from discontent to depression—a dark side we can easily downplay or dismiss. However, as professor and author Cal Newport observes, "We added new technologies to the periphery of our experience for minor reasons, then woke one morning to discover that they had colonized the core of our daily life. We didn't, in other words, sign up for the digital world in which we're currently entrenched; we seem to have stumbled backward into it."[2] While anyone could understandably use technology to keep in touch with a long-distance friend or to share information more efficiently, social media and smartphones go beyond that. As Newport says, "These technologies as a whole have managed to expand beyond the minor roles for which we initially adopted them. Increasingly, they dictate how we behave and how we feel, and somehow coerce us to use them more than we think is healthy, often at the expense of other activities we find more valuable. What's making us uncomfortable, in other words, is this feeling of losing control."

Consider a typical Saturday afternoon when I took my boys, seven and five at the time, out to the farmers' market for a bunch of vegetables they'd never eat while begging me to buy a sixty-dollar flower pot. With vegetable-laden canvas bags in tow, we headed to the real highlight of the morning: the local cafe that serves great cinnamon buns, even better coffee, and chic juice boxes. The kids ran to the back for the large checkerboard, and we started a never-ending checkers game with our drinks and "breakfast" at hand. Both boys were deeply concerned about preserving their checker pieces, and there were approximately forty-seven times when I could have been tempted to check my phone for new emails, hockey articles, hockey tweets, or social media notifications. In fact, checking my phone was a common part of our Saturday mornings at one time, when I would turn the boys loose with baked goods and a game and check my phone every three minutes—or less. Finally, I realized that I needed to cut myself off from my compulsive phone usage while with my kids. First, I deleted all social media apps from my phone. Then I added a usage tracker called Moment. Finally, I realized that I just needed to leave the phone in the car to break the habit once and for all.

Our digital devices and social media apps are limiting our ability to concentrate, to have conversations, to eat dinner with our families or friends, and to practice spirituality because they distract us, eat up valuable time, and train us to crave stimulation, affirmation, and passive amusement. Screen time estimates range between one to four hours per day for most smartphone users.[3] That doesn't even include time spent on a computer. Spending that many hours of our waking lives each day looking at our smartphones in addition to other screens is bound to affect us, and mountains of research studies suggest that it is.[4] One study led by psychologist Larry Rosen tracked how often high school students opened their phones daily and found that "participants had gone from unlocking their phones about 56 times a day in 2016 to 73 times a day in 2018."[5] Once we've connected to our digital devices, social media apps and sites like Twitter and Instagram are designed with infinite scrolling so that we're never truly done reviewing posts, while YouTube autoplays the next video and the next and the next. From hindering our ability to concentrate to leaving us feeling sad or isolated to stealing our time with binge-watching

or infinite scrolling, technology promised to make us more efficient and connected but comes with a steep price. The costs
to our mental health, relationships, and spirituality warrant re-
considering our exuberance over the moment a guy in a black
mock turtleneck introduced the first iPhone.

While I may take a walk next to that rustling field or pause
to glance up at the sky with a vague awareness of God, the truth
is that I have a digital device in my back pocket or the stroller,
if not in my hands, that has been designed to be irresistible,
compulsive, and consuming. I began using it because I believed
I could do *good* things with it, but its many steep costs make it
hard to do *better* things for my mental, relational, and spiritual
health. When I manage to leave my various screens behind on
their charging shelf at home, I try to look at the field down the
street from our house for a moment when the sun sets each
evening. The glowing pink, red, and yellow colors of the sunset
are just about the holiest thing I can find in this world. There's
something about that time of day, the brilliance before the fad-
ing, the majesty of a day ending no matter what transpired, and
the inevitable letting go as night quietly overtakes everything.
On clear evenings, I try to spend a few moments looking up at
the stars, but more often than not, I only look at the stars on
the nights when I'm taking out the garbage.

Why can't I manage to routinely step outside for a star-filled
night without being prompted by a full garbage can?

You may feel this tension as well. I suspect that being present in the moment feels so challenging in part because I live
each day plugged in to my smartphone and computer, engaging with social media and accessing unlimited information.
I have unlearned stillness and silence. The dopamine-driven
joy of a new message notification from a friend or the buzz

of affirmation offered by social media can pull me out of just about any moment. As I experimented with deleting apps from my devices, setting up social media blocks, blocking Internet access altogether on my phone or computer, and extending the time of these blocks from thirty minutes to five hours or more at a time, I saw how digital technology drained my attention and time.

This hasn't always been my approach to digital technology. I was an early adopter of blogging and social media, immersing myself in Facebook in particular at the urging of my first publisher's publicity department. I have kept in touch with some dear friends via social media over the years, and I clearly recall initially marveling over the ease of using social media apps on my new smartphone and tablet. I could access my network of friends, colleagues, and experts anytime I wanted! Soon I began to access that network all the time. Before too long, I wasn't just connecting with my friends constantly. I was spending my days worrying and fuming over the latest outrage, debate, threat, or controversy I found on social media. A single disconcerting tweet could send my anxiety, never stellar to begin with, into a tailspin.

The more I examined my use of these devices, the more I noticed how they fragmented my attention for my family and friends, decreased my ability to focus on work (or anything else, really), trained my brain to crave stimulation rather than the silence of prayer, and depleted the amount of time I had for enjoyable activities such as gardening, reading, or running (maybe use air quotes around "enjoyable" for that last one). All the good things in my life—from spiritual practices to time with my family to meaningful work and leisure projects—suffered because of my devices and social media use.

Our devices and social media have the power to shape us into a particular kind of people: distracted by many thoughts, reactive, compulsive, and impatient. Many of us are beginning to ask ourselves, Is that the kind of people we want to be? And if not, what can we do about it?

THE NEED FOR RESTORATION

No one picks up a smartphone with the intent of making their life more difficult or fragmented. We're all trying to cope with the challenges of life, to feel better, to make connections with people, to help others, and to get our work or daily tasks done a little more efficiently. Digital technology makes big promises in all those areas, and most Americans are immersed in it because of those promises. Smartphones and social media are now major fixtures of our days. Among American adults in 2019, 28 percent were online almost constantly (more than "several times a day") and 45 percent went online daily. Among the 86 percent of Americans who had a smartphone or other digital device, 32 percent were online almost constantly.[6] When it comes to general media use, such as watching television and using mobile phones, Americans spend an average of eleven hours per day consuming media.[7]

Even if we know that heavy smartphone usage is one of the forces in our lives that's consuming precious hours every week, many users either remain unaware of just how much time is lost or simply don't know where to start cutting back, since smartphones have become essential tools in our lives, carried around for every moment.[8] Rates of depression and anxiety drop and overall happiness and well-being increase when we cut back on our use of smartphones and social media.[9] But limiting technology use may have significance beyond simple improvements to well-being.

Our ability to be fully present for spiritual practices may be deeply limited by the ways technology impairs our ability to focus or to be still during a short period of solitude. Silence and solitude have long been essential aspects of Christian spirituality. We could list the solitude of wilderness encounters with God, prophetic ministries grounded in the wilderness, the teaching of Jesus to pray in solitude where only God sees us, the desert mothers and fathers who disengaged from the controversies of their time to seek God without hindrance, and the history of monks and nuns pursuing prayer in silence. We may well say that losing the ability to be alone may mean losing an essential part of Christian prayer and other spiritual practices. Prayer, meditation, and quietly waiting on God thrive in stillness, silence, and patient discipline—three things that digital formation counters with notifications, stimulation, and immediate gratification through feedback loops.

Longtime blogger Andrew Sullivan may offer some of the most pressing warnings about immersing ourselves in today's digital technology.[10] Rather than enhancing his real life with online interactions, he realized that he had traded his real-life interactions for online connections. He writes,

> I realized I had been engaging—like most addicts—in a form of denial. I'd long treated my online life as a supplement to my real life, an add-on, as it were. Yes, I spent many hours communicating with others as a disembodied voice, but my real life and body were still here. But then I began to realize, as my health and happiness deteriorated, that this was not a both-and kind of situation. It was either-or. Every hour I spent online was not spent in the physical world.[11]

In other words, we are training ourselves to exist in an alternate reality. While that alternate reality can certainly augment the real world in important ways, it can ultimately become a trade-off, keeping us from being fully present in our bodies and in the present moment.

Disembodied technology can devastate incarnate spirituality. How can we experience "God with us" if we aren't even aware of ourselves in the present moment?

Perhaps spiritual formation can coexist alongside the demands of digital formation, but technology of every kind is designed to take over and to destroy its limits. French philosopher Jacques Ellul, author of the 1954 book *The Technological Society*, worried that human dignity was suffering from idolizing a mechanized, technical society rather than using machines within humane boundaries and goals. Concerned that governments and corporations would exploit people through complex machines and mechanized systems, Ellul shared that technology created a way of thinking and interacting with the world that is mechanized in its outlook,[12] an approach Ellul called "technique" that values "absolute efficiency" above all else, posing a threat to the priorities that could lead to the flourishing of humanity.[13] While machines are an example of this commitment to efficiency that Ellul describes, this approach to the world becomes a mind-set for everything. Ellul clarifies his thinking by noting, "Wherever a technological factor exists, it results, almost inevitably, in mechanization: technique transforms everything it touches into a machine."[14] As a result, the efficiency of the process becomes more important than what we see in the final results or in the cost to humanity. As long as the efficient process is "sound" and "elegant," such as the sleek and easy-to-use design of an iPhone, we don't have to look too hard at its downside.

At a time of extreme optimism about the promise of technology and science to solve the world's problems, Ellul experienced firsthand the destruction brought by machines in the Second World War as he participated in the French resistance and then witnessed the faith that society placed in technology throughout the postwar years. A dedicated Christian who was immersed in Bible studies, home church meetings, ecological advocacy, and work with juvenile youth, Ellul urged his generation to turn a wary eye to the negative changes brought by unlimited optimism in technology. As Ellul saw some of his contemporaries struggle to respond constructively to the exploitation of people by machines and complex systems, he urged a smaller, more local approach to activism and is credited with coining the saying "Think globally, act locally"—a hopeful path forward that we'll revisit in the final chapter.

While there are endless opportunities for maintaining relationships over long distances or promoting a business on the cheap through smartphones and social media, the nature of digital technology today extends beyond its helpful utility. Technology is intentionally designed to be addictive and immersive. It endlessly pushes toward greater efficiency and speed—enhancing its appeal as a competitive edge. Technology is supposed to be hard to put down because fresh, endless posts are waiting with a simple swipe up, feedback is provided in measured doses, the next video is always ready to go, and notification pings ensure you never have to miss anything ever.

Our social media feeds are more likely to show us combative, extreme, and divisive content because such posts drive engagement that gets more responses and comments. As much as I try to avoid divisive discussions on social media, I usually don't have to scroll far before I see reactions to the latest out-rage, such as a celebrity pastor's bad take on politics, sexuality, or abusive church leadership. It doesn't help that some entities have gamed the system with dubious posts that are boosted by trolls or automated bots programmed to promote certain content. It's true that we can find colleagues, customers, friends, or family on social media, but we may be losing something valuable as we immerse ourselves in these distracting means of "connection" that could also hinder these same relationships. If we fail to take the design and impact of digital devices and social media seriously, we may lose the ability to be present, to focus, to be comfortable in silence, to maintain control over our emotions, and to value solitude.

If I were asked to describe what spiritual formation looks like, I might say that it involves patience, focus, silence, solitude, stillness, community, and regular practice. Centering prayer helps us release distracting thoughts with a prayer word so that we can become present for God. Whether practicing centering prayer or silent breathing in solitude, the experience of contemplative prayer, which is the interior work by the loving presence of God, is typically associated with a measure of stillness and awareness of God in the present moment. Consider a few descriptions of Christian spiritual formation and healthy spiritual practices and how they may be diminished by technology and social media:

Renovaré, an ecumenical Christian group that nurtures spiritual formation, offers the following definition: "Spiritual Formation is a process, but it is also a journey through which we open our hearts to a deeper connection with God."[15]

In *Invitation to a Journey: A Road Map for Spiritual Formation*, author M. Robert Mulholland writes, "Spiritual formation is a process of being conformed to the image of Christ for the sake of others."[16]

Theologian Howard Thurman writes, "We must find sources of strength and renewal for our own spirits, lest we perish. . . . First, we must learn to be quiet, to settle down in one spot for a spell."[17]

Author Cynthia Bourgeault simplifies our transformation in centering prayer to this simple practice:

Resist no thought
Retain no thought
React to no thought
Return to the sacred word.[18]

Words such as *journey*, *process*, and *quiet* are all frequently mentioned in conjunction with spiritual formation, and yet technology has trained us to choose the quick hit of affirmation or connection, the ideas put before us in the present, and short-term stimulation and interaction over the long-term benefits of silence. As technology, media, and social media occupy such large chunks of our lives every day, it's understandable that we struggle to make space for prayer, let alone to focus on prayer and other spiritual formation practices. The habits and expectations of technology and social media run directly counter to the practices and slow growth processes that make up the bread and butter of spiritual formation. We need to stop feeling guilty or hopeless about any struggles we may have in this area. We have a lot working against us.

Most of us don't experience spiritual transformation in an instant. It's a gradual, lifelong process. There may be flash-bang conversions or "deliverance" moments that send us leaping forward, but even then, we may feel that we are generally moving forward at a barely perceptible pace as we are shaped by God's influence in our lives. The process of spiritual transformation is often slow and rarely spectacular, taking place in the mundane habits and choices we make each day.

The trouble today is that we're typically carrying the single most powerful tool for a very different kind of formation in our pockets. Our homes are dotted with digital devices that demand our attention and promise things we previously never could have imagined possible. Using them feels good—until it feels too good and we cannot stop inviting them into our lives, even carrying these devices into holy moments and sacred space. Digital formation is training us to interact with others, with information, and even with spirituality in ways that are often detrimental and at the very least inadequate.

A few years after Jacques Ellul sounded his warning about optimism for technology and its possibilities for causing harm among those who were not powerful or wealthy, a monk in America harbored his own concerns about the ways machines could limit human flourishing, let alone interfere with prayer. Thomas Merton, a Trappist monk and bestselling author of *The Seven Storey Mountain*, happened upon Ellul's *The Technological Society* in the 1960s and praised it as prophetic, logical, and full of firecrackers—the ultimate Merton compliment.[19] As Merton compiled his reflections on the challenges facing humanity in his groundbreaking book *Conjectures of a Guilty Bystander*, Ellul's influence shines through: "Technology has its own ethic of expediency and efficiency," writes Merton. "What *can* be done efficiently *must* be done in the most efficient way. . . . Even the long-term economic interests of society, or the basic needs of man himself, are not considered when they get in the way of technology."[20] While I had been reading Merton's writing about prayer for several years, such as *New Seeds of Contemplation* and *Thoughts in Solitude*, the despair of social media, the stakes of current events, and my struggle to turn away from both prompted me to read *Conjectures of a Guilty Bystander* with fresh eyes. Long before engineers wired the digital devices we have come to rely on today, Merton saw how destructive modern technology could become for our souls, let alone our ability to pray, if we failed to see technology's influence with clarity and place appropriate boundaries around it.

Merton adopted a high view of humanity as God's beloved creation and encouraged his contemporaries to seek the well-being of their neighbors in all facets of life, including the use of technology. Merton was less concerned about efficiency, speed, or the cost-saving measures of technology because he spent so much time examining its impact. Rather than serving reason, humanity, or God, Merton believed the following about modern technology: "Becoming autonomous, existing only for itself, it imposes upon man its own irrational demands, and threatens to destroy him." Merton was not opposed to technology in all its manifestations; he even flew to Asia to meet with other religious leaders. (Ironically, Merton died on this trip because of technology after accidentally electrocuting himself in Thailand.) His concerns addressed the practical experiences of people, let alone the monks seeking to pray at the Abbey of Gethsemani as tractors roared in nearby fields. These machines made the monastery more profitable but dramatically changed the kind of work the monks did, as well as the atmosphere of the abbey. How would this change to manual labor alter the way he and other monks prayed?

As digital formation takes root, we may lose touch with God's life-giving presence that can shape our lives and reconnect us with the kind of flourishing and freedom God intended for each of us. Seeking a path forward through the distraction and confusion that technology brought to my spiritual practices, I found that Merton, aided by the insights of Ellul, could offer a good deal of wisdom for us as we seek a humane path through the buzzes, notifications, and altercations of our technology-driven times. If the makers of digital technology are largely driven to advance their devices and apps without the well-being of users in mind, Merton and Ellul offer a clear-eyed, Christian response that will help us preserve space in our minds and daily schedules for prayer and silence before God. However, if they are going to help us, we need to first understand the scale of what we're up against.

IT'S NOT JUST UP TO YOU

The focus of many Christians at the time of this writing has been on personal responsibility, habits, and setting better boundaries for their smartphone and app use. The book *The Tech-Wise Family* is an example of this approach that aims to empower users to make better choices—and does an excellent job of laying out the social media landscape for families while providing helpful solutions, ones that our family also uses. However, self-discipline is only one way to gain control over our device and app use. Looking at the full complexity of technological formation can reveal the ways our apps and devices, by their design and usage, keep us hooked and even override our best intentions. Judith Donath, author of *The Social Machine: Designs for Living Online*, commented, "Keeping people in a continual state of anxiety, anger, fear, or just haunted by an inescapable, nagging sense that everyone else is better off than they are can be very profitable."[21] We aren't up against neutral technology tools that merely help us accomplish particular goals and only have a dark side because of our errors or poor habits. We're up against a variety of challenges: a wider effort by digital technology companies to hack our minds and desires, information on social media that manipulates us, and a consumer culture that values selling products which lead to comfort and indulgence, all while facing the age-old challenge to develop better habits and make better choices with our time. Personal choice is part of the puzzle, but we are bound to fail if we don't consider the design, purpose, and ad-driven ecosystem of digital technology and social media in planning our response.

Our self-control is a limited resource that can wear out like a muscle. As we encounter addictive devices and apps that trigger our desires for connection, accomplishment, and affirmation, we'll lose almost every time if we aren't prepared for the full onslaught coming our way. Sure, we can make better choices as the day begins and the sweet aroma of coffee drifts from our kitchens. However, it's much harder to resist the appeal of our screens and social media at the low points in the afternoon or in the tired, waning hours of the day. Even with our best habits in place, we may need stronger countermeasures to resist the daily tug of social media. In fact, I would argue that we need to take more drastic and intentional steps to counter the designs of engineers who are using the best of technological innovation, persuasive design research (yes, there is such a thing), and habit-formation techniques to capture our attention.

I have no intention of telling people to stop using their phones completely, to use a flip phone, to dumpster dive as resistance to the consumer economy, or to replace social media with letter writing. Rather, I want us to restore an element of free choice in our use of technology, specifically creating more space to choose things that are good for us (and others), like spiritual practices and serving our neighbors. If you don't know how an app is designed to capture your attention and keep you hooked, are you really making a free choice when you feel compelled to pick it up, struggle to put it down, or live in fear of leaving home without your phone? Are we truly aware of how our ability to pay attention and to focus is being impaired by our smartphone and social media use? Our current situation is such that it's hard to choose prayer or to practice spiritual disciplines in part because of how technology has trained and rewired us.

The Christians in my circles are especially prone to beating themselves up over their failure to regulate their use of technology. We tend to be an optimistic, bootstrapping religious subculture that believes in the power of the individual to rise above challenges. Our notions of sin and personal responsibility can sometimes make it difficult for us to speak about harmful systems, addiction, or manipulation. While social media and smartphone use fall under the category of behavior addictions rather than substance addictions, we are mistaken if we underestimate how powerful behavioral addictions can be. Digital technology's formative influence is so troubling because it capitalizes, literally, on our good desires for connection, relationships, and personal expression.

There is a more holistic and realistic approach that I hope to forge, taking seriously the designs of digital formation while suggesting ways to develop habits that make space for God and others. The more we are formed by digital technology, the harder it will become to muster the focus and time for spiritual practices. However, if we are informed and intentional about our digital device use, I believe that we can make space to reconnect with God in deeper, life-giving ways.

For Christians living in a world of digital devices and social media, our primary concern isn't efficiency, speed, or even expanding our influence and connections. We are first and foremost concerned with our identities as beloved children of God, created in God's image and blessed by Christ becoming incarnate among humanity. Our souls are renewed because of the presence of Christ in our lives—the vine that we are connected to as branches that wither when relying on ourselves or any other source of support. Anything that draws us away from the vine will leave us fragmented and disconnected. If we have any hope of reconnecting with the life of Christ, our vine and our sustenance, we need to see how technology itself, even if we intend to use it for good ends, prevents the flourishing of humanity.

. . . INVITATION TO RECONNECT . . . .

Consider your relationship to silence and stillness. Choose one way to add a few minutes of silence each day. For instance, drive to work in silence.

What makes it hard to experience silence and stillness?

If you could change your use of a smartphone or social media in one way right now, how would you change it?

When you look at how much money Facebook and Google and YouTube print every day, it's all about building the user base. Building engagement was important, and they didn't care about the nature of engagement. Or maybe they did, but in a bad way. The more people who got angry on those sites—Reddit especially—the more engagement you would get.

—ELLEN PAO, FORMER CEO OF REDDIT

ONE

The Goal of Digital Formation

I deleted Facebook from my phone and my tablet. I blocked the Facebook news feed on my computer. I limited my combined time on Twitter and Facebook to less than twenty minutes each day with the StayFocusd extension on my browser.

Yet on my birthday, I wanted to keep up with the happy birthday messages from friends, family, and colleagues, so I installed the Facebook app on my tablet for the day, checked on the well wishes, and then started scrolling down for updates from friends, interesting articles, funny memes, and informative videos. It was just like old times.

While I cleaned up after breakfast, my son waited for me to help with a Lego project. After stacking the dishes precariously on the drying rack, I took a "quick break" to watch a video in my feed. My son, still waiting in the other room, finally called out, "Daddy, why aren't you coming to help me?"

I deleted the app and haven't put the app back on my tablet since.

Sure, Facebook helps us see what other people are up to, but perhaps it is too optimistic to say it "connects" us. Did I make any connections as I scrolled through the twenty or so updates on my tablet while my son waited in the other room? What happened to my connection with my son while I was "engaged" on Facebook? Had I drawn closer in a significant way to anyone in my circles of friends, family, and colleagues while scrolling through my news feed, or had I whittled away ten minutes that could have been given to my son with focused attention? I'm not so sure that I am a better, more connected person because of the phone in my pocket that instantly opens a world of social media apps and communication options like texting.

Why have I felt the need to continue removing apps from devices, to place strict limits on my social media use, and to guard my time so strictly? Is it merely a matter of my own weaknesses? Or am I trying to counteract something that goes beyond my desires and habits?

We don't necessarily need to wade through research studies or the expert opinions of psychologists to prove that devices and social media apps are designed to become invasive, habit-forming, and compulsive—if not a behavioral addiction at times. Many of the people who design digital technology and social media have publicly stated that their products are designed to be toxic, addicting, and manipulative, depriving users of choice and free time through habit-forming feedback loops where the reactions and notifications become the rewards to keep using social media. Digital devices and social media certainly can't "control" the people who use their products, but they can dramatically change how people feel and what many people think, say, and do.

Formation and manipulation has always been the goal, regardless of any upsides that digital technology offers.

Some former Silicon Valley executives and engineers have become whistleblowers about the harm their devices cause. A significant number of them have formed the Center for Humane Technology (www.humanetech.com), an organization that both exposes the dark side of digital technology and offers humane design alternatives. Every feature, from the colors of apps to the ways notifications are revealed to the social feedback loop of social media and other apps on smartphones, shares the ultimate goal of capturing attention for as long as possible. These former insiders believe that technology isn't designed with human flourishing in mind, but rather is designed to form us into regular, if not compulsive, users for the sake of collecting data[1] and profits by training us to always have a reason to use our devices, invading every still and quiet moment of our days.[2] The goals of technology formation are often at odds with spiritual formation, which thrives in stillness and quiet.

Shane Harris, the founder of the Center for Humane Technology and formerly of Google, shared that a smartphone with social media apps becomes like a slot machine in your pocket, forever promising a quick fix of good feelings from a notification, a new video that's ready to go, or a friend's update. Leah Pearlman, the cocreator of the red notification button on Facebook, literally had to stop using Facebook because the red notification button was too appealing and became linked to her self-esteem and daily moods (as of this writing, these notifications appear as a red bubble on top of a bell on the Facebook home page). Although Pearlman knew how the notification works, she realized how dependent she had become. "When I need validation—I go to check Facebook," she said.

"I'm feeling lonely, 'Let me check my phone.' I'm feeling inse-cure, 'Let me check my phone.' . . . I noticed that I would post something that I used to post and the 'like' count would be way lower than it used to be." Pearlman didn't hesitate to use the word *addiction* in assessing herself: "Suddenly, I thought I'm actually also kind of addicted to the feedback."[3]

The phones we carry and the apps we use on them are not charities designed to make the world a better place. They ex-ist to make money for their companies, and they offer free services to collect data that can later be monetized, tracking which websites you visit, where you live, and which activities you prefer. Before the birth of our first child, I never consid-ered my "good fortune" that all these incredible promotions and coupons for diapers, baby clothes, and nursery furniture miraculously showed up just when we were shopping for items in his nursery. Making a profit is certainly companies' right, but let's not kid ourselves about their ultimate designs or the means they use. Their chosen way to collect more data and to increase profits is to make apps and devices as irresistible as possible. If I feel a constant need to check my phone or tablet for notifications, information, connections, or messages, it's likely that at least some of the time I'll stick around to scroll through updates, view a few ads, and perhaps even click through a few links and begin a kind of rabbit trail that will almost certainly be less rewarding than initially imagined, leav-ing me likely to keep checking back for more updates. At the very least, I've provided some data to the company to be used for future ads.

Despite these concerning trends about social media and dig-ital devices, there are benefits. I have learned so much through the writings of activists on Twitter about racism, immigration, and the experiences of people of color in America. Facebook groups have kept me in touch with many of my writing colleagues when it would be challenging to correspond and interact so easily over email or, shudder, *phone calls*. The benefits of social media and my smartphone prevent me from a complete digital blackout, but that only drives home the urgency of placing boundaries around digital tools sooner than later.

Our challenge today is that we have more opportunities to have more connections with more people and to communicate in more ways and with more access to more information, to the point that we may be undermining our goals of intimate relationships and meaningful activities. There are many good things to gain from social media, but because social media and digital devices are designed with different goals than our own, we may end up fulfilling the wishes of engineers and executives rather than our own. Can we use social media in a way that maximizes its benefits without undermining our own goals of spiritual formation and intimate relationships? It's certainly possible to pursue a kind of "digital minimalism" that preserves space for spiritual practices and real-life relationships, but only if we learn how social media is designed and how it influences the ways we interact with each other.

THE BENEFITS ARE THE BAIT

We don't have to look far to find the benefits of digital devices and social media:

Instagram presents itself as a tool for visual expression.

Facebook assures us that it's connecting the world.

Twitter claims to be the fastest way to find out what's going on.

YouTube shares useful videos and entertainment.

Snapchat offers consistent connection with friends.

There is a measure of truth to these claims. I follow quite a few artists and photographers on Instagram. I keep in touch with distant family, friends, and colleagues on Facebook. I learn a great deal from activists, journalists, and experts on Twitter. My kids love a good hockey highlights video on YouTube. I'll have to take Snapchat users at their word . . .

Speaking personally, social media is pretty great for an introverted writer who has colleagues and readers scattered all over. I have developed and maintained important relationships and sold plenty of books thanks to social media. If anyone has a reason to praise social media and the digital devices that make social media and other apps even easier to use, it's someone like myself. I am quite happy writing in the back corner of a cafe, drinking the cheapest cup of coffee, and occasionally sending out social media posts for "book publicity."

In my family, we make FaceTime calls on our tablet with distant family members, and each week we post pictures from our phones to shared photo groups to keep grandparents, aunts, and uncles in the loop about our kids. When I need to fix something, YouTube helps me make it less bad before calling a legitimate repair professional for help. It would be incorrect to say that these devices and apps are a net loss. They wouldn't be so pervasive and readily embraced if they didn't offer immediate and visible benefits. The problem is that we remain unaware of the true purpose and design that drives their darker sides. Even worse, when we experience the negative aspects of these devices and apps, we tend to blame ourselves for not being disciplined, determined, or wise enough to click away, to turn off the phone, or to put the tablet down. These apps and devices are incorrectly considered neutral tools that will make life easier and more efficient, and so we make the mistake of believing we only have ourselves to blame if we misuse them.

Such optimism about technology filtered down to us from the people who also had the most to gain from it. The founders of technology argued that their products would make our world more connected and would empower more people to gain more access to knowledge. While this optimism has been true in part, Ellen Pao, former CEO of Reddit, writes about the idealism and the homogeneity that surrounded the early days of the Internet and social media in general:

> I think two things are at the root of the present crisis. One was the idealistic view of the internet—the idea that this is the great place to share information and connect with like-minded people. The second part was the people who started these companies were very homogeneous. You had one set of experiences, one set of views, that drove all of the platforms on the internet. So the combination of this belief that the internet was a bright, positive place and the very similar people who all shared that view ended up creating platforms that were designed and oriented around free speech.[4]

The truth is, information has never been more accessible, but fake stories and misinformation have also never been so pervasive or so targeted at the individuals most inclined to believe them.[5] Our family and friends may be extremely accessible on social media, but we are also at greater risk of arguments and divisions over news stories and social issues. We can access unprecedented information, but are we too distracted and unfocused to process it? We can share our work and creative pursuits on social media, but these same tools become time-draining distractions that offer an escape from reality and the challenges we face each day—the very things that may inspire our artistic and creative projects. We have wonderful new ways to share messages with many people, empowering previously over-looked voices, but those same platforms are also infected with angry users lacking empathy, as well as with trolls and bots who unleash harassment in unceasing waves. It's as if every benefit we can list for digital technology or social media is paired with a steep cost.

Teens report significant anxiety over getting enough shares and likes on their photos, and since every gathering is meticulously documented, those who aren't present experience a sharp pain of missing out. For instance, one teenage user of Instagram shared, "I've had friends who have posted pictures they love, but when they only have 50 likes in the first hour within posting it, they delete it and say 'just wasn't getting the likes I thought it would.'"[6] Psychologist Jean M. Twenge shares that behaviors and emotional states among teens reached alarming, unprecedented lows starting in 2012 when smartphones became pervasive and ownership surpassed 50 percent of the population. Twenge had never seen such a change in any generation, dating back to the 1930s, and as she merged interviews with teens and research studies, she could only conclude that smartphones have been severely harming mental health—which is exactly what the whistleblowers from Silicon Valley are telling us.[7]

At the root of our struggle to use social media and smartphones well are the very good qualities that make us human, relational beings created in God's image. We crave socializing, interaction, acceptance, and the simple joy of knowing we belong. However, social media and our weak digital connections can trick us into thinking that these connections are the real thing (or can promise more meaningful interactions than what's possible) and provide incentives to invest in digital connections at the expense of in-person interactions. Clinical psychologist and sociologist Sherry Turkle asks, "What if one of the things that technology wants is to exploit our disappointments and emotional vulnerabilities? When this is what technology wants, it wants to be a symptom. . . . Like all psychological symptoms, it obscures a problem by 'solving' it without addressing it."[8] Digital technology can supplement in-person connections and help maintain relationships over long distances, but the longing we feel for community, acceptance, and interaction is a craving for something beyond what we can find on a screen. Our devices and social media apps are best designed to supplement belonging to a group or finding support in a time of loss or struggle, not to stand in for the real presence of community and friends who can love and affirm us.

The problem with inhumane technology is that it exploits real needs and real pain with half measures and inadequate solutions that fail to address the root needs of community and belonging in our lives for the sake of collecting data and attention to turn a profit. Turkle warned in the early days of social media and smartphone technology that our enchantment with technology comes with a price. "We transgress not because we try to build the new but because we don't allow ourselves to consider what it disrupts or diminishes," she writes. "We are not in trouble because of invention but because we think it will solve everything."[9] In a short time these digital upstarts have presented themselves as indispensable regardless of the cost. For a more extreme example of technology's limitations, when a friend of ours suffered a medical emergency, her family used social media to share updates and to organize a fundraiser. However, that couldn't replace the people who showed up at her family's home to drop off meals, to provide childcare, and to take care of household projects. The in-person relationships were the most important, even if social media had its place. When it comes to our overuse of social media and smartphones, it's valid to ask whether technology truly serves us or whether we find ourselves serving technology to our own detriment.

After observing the impact of social media throughout the world, we have good cause to ask whether optimism about digital technology needs to be challenged more robustly. Injecting a measure of cynicism into the technological optimism of the 1960s, where some even developed plans to deliver mail via rockets amid fears of nuclear war,[10] Thomas Merton wrote, "We do not know if we are building a fabulously wonderful world or destroying all that we have ever had, all that we have achieved!" He went on to add about the misplaced optimism given to technology, "Man is all ready to become a god, and instead he appears at times to be a zombie."[11] Such words could have been written today about the ironic twist of digital technology and social media that promise more freedom while entangling us to the point that some fear life without their phones.

This feeling of dependence can give way to despair or resignation (or both) to the influence of smartphones and social media. Beyond the benefits that are clear to see, the smartphone has become an essential item in modern life that many of us believe we can't live without. What started as fun gadget that could make life easier and more convenient by blending a variety of tools together like a Swiss Army knife has turned into a kind of hostage situation where we feel bound to endure the device's negative impact lest we lose connection with our loved ones and friends.

This is where technology companies stand to really make some money.

YOU VERSUS A THOUSAND ENGINEERS

In 2007, psychologist B. J. Fogg taught a class in the Stanford Persuasive Technology Lab, where he merged his studies in habit formation with digital technology. He developed a behavior model (www.behaviormodel.org) that teaches that our habits come from the convergence of three forces: motivation, ability, and prompt (or "trigger"). If you can easily do something and you're motivated to do it, a simple prompt will result in action.

Several members of his class began designing third-party Facebook apps that attracted such high levels of engagement that they were soon selling banner ads for a significant profit. Students from his class went on to found Instagram (Kevin Systrom and Mike Krieger) and to take positions at Facebook, Google, and Uber. Although Fogg's technology and habit research had been used for positive ends, such as peacemaking, enjoying nature, or quitting smoking, its uncritical application to social media is, at best, consistent with the misplaced optimism for online connections at the time.[12]

While Fogg's method may also serve as a useful way to opt out of digital technology formation, the merging of technology and psychology is a crucial piece of the puzzle for understanding the challenges posed by social media and digital devices. Consider that social media users are already *motivated* to use these apps to connect with people and to be affirmed among their peers. The *ability* of an app is kept simple by engineers who have made them user-friendly and designed algorithms to make it easy to keep up with what appears most important or engaging. Notifications *prompt* app use by sending regular pings, pop-ups, and little red bubbles to remind users to return to the app, which they're already motivated to use for connection.

The red bubbles are especially critical for keeping users hooked. "Red," write P. W. Singer and Emerson Brooking, "is the color of agitation and psychological arousal, the mere glimpse of which can lead to a spike in heart rate. It feels *good* to make red things go away. Because notifications are purposefully vague until touched, following them can feel like opening a present."[13] Merton wrote, as if predicting the approach and impact of social media, about the confluence of technology and the consumer economy, "It is by means of technology that man the person, the subject of qualified and perfectible freedom, becomes quantified, that is, becomes part of a mass—mass [humanity]—whose only function is to enter anonymously into the process of production and consumption."[14] We now have the insights of psychology and technology working together to design apps and devices that are extremely difficult to resist because, for their creators, more consumption is always good for business.

Among the students in Fogg's class, Tristan Harris went on to enjoy a successful career at Google before raising alarms about the ethics of design being used to manipulate users. Harris shared in an interview how YouTube manages to hook us, even if we try to limit ourselves:

> I'm just going to watch this one video and then somehow, that's not what happens. You wake up from a trance three hours later and you say, "What the h*** just happened?" And it's because you didn't realize you had a supercomputer pointed at your brain. So when you open up that video you're activating Google's billions of dollars of computing power and they've looked at what has ever gotten 2 billion human animals to click on another video. And it knows way

more about what's going to be the perfect chess move to play against your mind. If you think of your mind as a chessboard, and you think you know the perfect move to play—I'll just watch this one video. But you can only see so many moves ahead on the chessboard. But the computer sees your mind and it says, "No, no, no. I've played a billion simulations of this chess game before on these other human animals watching YouTube," and it's going to win. . . . So it's not that we're completely losing human agency and you walk in to YouTube and it always addicts you for the rest of your life and you never leave the screen. But everywhere you turn on the internet there's basically a supercomputer pointing at your brain, playing chess against your mind, and it's going to win a lot more often than not.[15]

The autoplay feature on YouTube resembles the way that shows on Netflix automatically load so that viewers never have to stop bingeing on a show. Considering Fogg's approach to habit formation, the motivation for entertainment is present, the ability to watch the next show is already possible once you start viewing a series, and the prompt's trigger is pulled if you simply sit still. Harris understands both the human and the technological dynamics at play to keep YouTube viewers hooked. If companies won't back away from covertly using them, he hopes to at least give viewers enough information to make better decisions while challenging companies to make their technology more humane.

This idea of endless content possibilities isn't confined to YouTube. For instance, Facebook, Twitter, and Instagram each use an "infinite scroll" feature that serves up an endless stream of new images, updates, and videos. There is no bottom, no option to flip to another page if you follow enough people.

The process is slightly different from one social media company or app to another, but the ultimate goal is to always increase the time users spend on the app. Aza Raskin, the creator of the infinite scroll feature, shared, "Behind every screen on your phone, there are generally like literally a thousand engineers that have worked on this thing to try to make it maximally addicting."[16]

More importantly, we also need to look at what kinds of data these companies are collecting from us and what their ends are. While no one wants to deprive a company of a chance to turn an honest profit, certain practices are worthy of scrutiny. In an internal Facebook document leaked to *The Australian* newspaper, executives bragged to advertisers that they could detect when users felt depressed. Certain words, photo colorations, and angles were all associated with depression and other mental health issues. Teens who admitted that they "feel worthless" were among those noted by the social media giant. Did Facebook have the best interests of its users in mind, or was it seeking to exploit psychological vulnerabilities for the sake of profit?[17]

Such forays into mental health are nothing new for Facebook. A 2014 report found that it had manipulated the news feed of over 693,000 users to alter their moods.[18] This was done without their consent or even knowledge. How many Facebook users and their loved ones were influenced by this experiment in manipulation? While Facebook may offer legitimate opportunities for interaction and connection, it may also alter your mood and take valuable time from in-person relationships. Regardless of what we bring to our online interactions, there's also a near guarantee that we'll become angry or distraught by something we find on social media. As it turns out, extreme views and conflict are also really good for business if you're in the social media and digital device industry.

THE BEST FIGHT WINS

Depending on your point of view, there is nothing worse or better than watching a video of someone make a giant ice cream sundae while you exercise. For one point of view, ice cream undermines the health benefits of exercise; however, some, like Matt Inman of *The Oatmeal* comic, believe in running so that they can eat anything . . . like cake.[19] I'm in the former camp, so I found it a bit grating when my gym aired two months of the same interview at the same time with the same ice cream shop owner on the televisions next to the running track. Your guess is as good as mine why someone set the television to the same exact show for so long. The interview was part of a series called The Business of Going Viral, featuring absurd food marketing strategies such as colorful bagels, towering burgers, and sizzling waves of melted cheese on a plate. I got a good look at those ridiculously large sundaes that had ice cream, whipped cream, and toppings erupting out the top and streaming down the sides.

The segment showed customers snapping pictures of these monstrosities—and that, of course, is why this owner made absurdly large sundaes. My beloved childhood Happy Ending Sundae from Friendly's restaurant doesn't cut it in the world of viral advertising and social media. We all know what it's going to look like, so why bother snapping a selfie of yourself as you're about to dig into a rather ho-hum (but still delicious) sundae? Now, double the amount of ice cream, shoot sauces anywhere you please, empty out the can of whipped cream, cover it all with a box of cereal, and whip your phone out for a quick #foodstagram before half of it cascades to the floor. *That* is viral marketing.

Ironically, an insightful study of extreme and divisive views on issues such as healthcare and racism shared via social media also noted that even food pictures had become "extreme." It turns out that the research completely backs up the savvy strategies highlighted in that series about large ice cream sundaes. Embracing the pun for all it's worth, who wants just vanilla on their social media feed? We want the oddly unusual, the strongest statements, the brilliant clapback that "destroys" the other perspective, or the burn from the hottest take. Those hoping to attract attention have every incentive to take the low road, to push extreme perspectives, and to pick as many fights as they can bear. The content that gets the most engagement is often related to some kind of emotional reaction or conflict, and our own comments and shares may only fan their flames.[20]

Social media doesn't just make division more likely; the way it rewards popular content and engagement makes it almost inevitable. In sports, a radio personality may argue that a team's star player is actually a bum who should be traded. In politics, someone may argue that women aren't as effective in elected office as men. In religion, a pastor may argue that presumed Christians who disagree with his views aren't actually Christians after all. Whether these people believe what they're arguing becomes irrelevant in the flurry of responses and attention that surrounds their "bad take." The priority of many popular social media users is to stand out, and the best ways to stand out are to post often and to post something unique or unusual. The lazy but effective way to be unique or unusual is to operate on the extremes, the space where people say, "I can't believe he just posted that!" While it's certainly easy to draw a crowd by starting a fight, enough people are starting fights that those who want to stand out need to start fights in the most extreme, and noticeable, manner possible.

This is the central strategy of some politicians and political parties today that can control news cycles by endorsing the most extreme policies, fanning the flames of the worst rhetoric, and attacking the most vulnerable in the most brazen ways possible.[21] Politicians who rally their followers with chants of "Build the wall!" are not inviting us to think rationally and constructively about the refugee, migration, and asylum challenges of our times. They are fostering a combative siege mentality among the people who support their policies while baiting their opponents with a new extreme statement. Communication professor Robert Kozinets writes, "The algorithms that drive participation and attention-getting in social media, the addictive 'gamification' aspects such as likes and shares, invariably favored the odd and unusual. When someone wanted to broaden out beyond his or her immediate social networks, one of the most effective ways to achieve mass appeal turned out to be by turning to the extreme."[22] Kozinets found that "smartphones and web applications were increasing people's passions while also driving them to polarizing extremes." He adds, "The basic engagement mechanisms of popular social media sites like Facebook drive people to think and communicate in ever more extreme ways."[23]

Nation-states and corporations are investing in trolls (someone who deliberately attacks others or disrupts conversations online) and divisive figures, infiltrating both sides of already divisive issues to drive a larger wedge into society and create more instability and division. The Army of Jesus Facebook page was created and managed by a foreign nation to sow division among Christians during the 2016 election,[24] while a Twitter account posing as the Tennessee Republican Party was also a complete fabrication by a foreign nation.[25] In the wake of a controversial police shooting, trolls then entered into legitimate discussions and activism in order to sow chaos, creating accounts such as the @blacktivist Twitter handle.[26] It's not just that activists were being targeted and harassed by trolls. There were trolls posing as activists who sought to divide and polarize the activists from within their ranks. Some trolls even used their deceptive social media accounts to plan protests that people attended as either participants or counterprotestors.[27] Of course the planners were nowhere to be seen at the events themselves. Even for those who weren't following these fake accounts, many thousands of social media users were also exposed to ads run by these troll-backed accounts.[28] At the very least, social media platforms were not willing to face this problem, even denying it when overwhelming evidence pointed to the contrary.[29] It was only in 2018 and 2019 that social media companies became more proactive in removing fake accounts sowing disinformation and division.

Venture capitalist Roger McNamee, who has deep ties to Silicon Valley leaders, including Mark Zuckerberg and Cheryl Sandberg, noted that brands had recognized the impact of social media on their customers. As McNamee put it, one brand essentially told Facebook, "Your platform's too good. You're basically harming our customers. Because you're manipulating what they think. And more importantly, you're manipulating what they feel. You're causing so much outrage that they become addicted to outrage." The dopamine we get from outrage, noted McNamee, "is just so addictive." In his estimation, social media companies are "basically trying to trigger fear and anger

THE GOAL OF DIGITAL FORMATION / **53**

to get the outrage cycle going, because outrage is what makes you be more deeply engaged. You spend more time on the site and you share more stuff. Therefore, you're going to be exposed to more ads, and that makes you more valuable."[30]

The starting point of anger may be genuine conflict, a manufactured conflict, or the regular ebb and flow of reacting to media online, but the result is that emotional triggers are a key factor in keeping us hooked on social media and our devices. Whether we want to follow up on a conflict, to catch up with friends, or to simply have a bit of distraction to disconnect from boredom or the low points of the day, technology and social media are hardly neutral forces in our lives. They have their own agenda that extends well beyond keeping us connected.

TECHNOLOGY IS NOT NEUTRAL

From what I know of the Christian subculture in America, we tend to think of technology as a neutral tool that can be used for good or for bad. For instance, a hammer is a simple tool that can be used to pound a nail or to pound a finger—not that I would know anything about the latter. The former is a good use of the tool, while the latter is a bad use of the tool. The positive or negative effects of the hammer, assuming it's constructed well, rests completely in the hands of the user.

Running with this example to an absurd extreme, let's imagine that a hammer is a tool much like a smartphone. Imagine that the brand-new iHammer has a particularly sleek and pleasing design that is marketed as the true tool of a real professional seeking to gain an edge in the quest for upward mobility. The type of hammer you buy is deemed to be a vital factor in how you present yourself to others—the iHammer is presented as the best, most professional-looking hammer on the market. It even makes it easier to use all your other tools. However, to the surprise of many customers, the new, sleek iHammer prompts many of its owners to carry it everywhere. In fact, they can't stop thinking about hammering nails into things, because it feels so good to use it, and they need to tell their friends about it. They need to hammer nails first thing in the morning and often stay up late at night hammering things. They can hardly have a conversation because they're always hammering nails into things. While the presence of the iHammer was originally praised as a step forward for a society of "handy people" always ready to fix something, negative reports of extreme iHammer activity begin to surface. Restaurants even report that iHammer users have left tables full of hammered nails, forks, and even a spoon in one ambitious case. The iHammer users admit that they sometimes go a little overboard, but add that hammers are extremely useful tools. Hammers build houses, after all! Never mind that houses built with an iHammer are often over budget and a painter's worst nightmare because they're practically covered with nails.

As absurd as this scenario may be, it's not too far removed from our current situation, where many argue that digital devices and social media apps are neutral tools even though depression, suicide, and anxiety rates skyrocketed just as these devices became pervasive in society. Former designers, executives, and venture capitalists who know the devices and their strategies intimately have been sounding the alarm for years about the downside of digital technology for users. While we have no choice in living with digital technology, we also should be realistic about the kind of world it has created.

Our society is changing dramatically because of technology, thanks to both its efficiencies and deficiencies. While Merton was resigned to the technological future, he also offers a compelling statement about what we should prepare for:

> There is no escaping technology. . . . It isn't just that we have got a lot of machines. But that the entire life of man is being totally revolutionized by technology. This has to be made very clear. We are not at all living just in an age where we have more tools, more complicated tools, and things are a little more efficient, that kind of thing. It's a totally new kind of society we're living in.[31]

Technology is shaping us and our society whether we realize it or not. Besides the designs of technology, we need to clearly see the changes brought by digital formation before we can suggest ways to counteract it with practices that can help us reconnect with God and with each other.

. . . INVITATION TO RECONNECT . . . .

With B. J. Fogg's three steps for developing a habit in mind, consider how they relate to your own digital device and social media use. There's typically overlap between each category:

- What motivates you to use social media, a smartphone, or both? (For example, keeping in touch with friends and family, professional networking.)

- What makes it easy for you to use social media, a smartphone, or both? (For example, I carry my phone with me everywhere, and social media is the first thing I see on my screen.)

- What prompts you to use social media, a smartphone, or both? (For example, whenever I'm bored or tired, it's a good distraction.)

If you would like to cut back on your smartphone or social media use, consider these questions:

- How can you remove motivation to use it as often?

- How can you make it harder to access?

- How can you replace social media and smartphone prompts with prompts to do something else?

We are the prisoners of every urgency. In this way we so completely lose all perspective and sense of values that we are no longer able to estimate correctly what even the most immediate consequences of our actions may turn out to be.

—THOMAS MERTON

How Digital Formation Changes Us

If I placed a new, brand-name smartphone on the table and said, "This is for you," I wouldn't have to say much else to persuade most people to grab it and run.

No one needs to make a case for the benefits of technology. From smartphones to social media apps, we are surrounded by people who use them. We certainly wouldn't spend so much money on smartphones or invest so much time in social media if we didn't believe we were getting something of value from them. Yet when we pause long enough to look at who we are becoming and how we are spending our time, there are real concerns about the ways social media and smartphones are affecting our lives. They are shaping our lives in ways that many of us aren't even recognizing. Perhaps we could benefit by listing our reasons for using a smartphone and other digital devices and then listing how we spend our time with them each day. Do our original intentions match our current usage?

In a larger view of technology today, our digital devices are a symptom of our attachment to efficiency, moving faster, doing more, and always developing better processes to break new limits. The words of Jacques Ellul about our commitment to efficiency and turning everything into a kind of mechanical process ring through in Thomas Merton's writings about technology. Merton argues, "We are concerned only with 'practicality'—'efficiency': that is, with means, not with ends. And therefore we are more and more concerned only with immediate consequences."[1] For a simple example, we could compare the efficiency of a car with the slower speed of taking a bike on a path. While the car appears to be the obvious choice because it's faster and more efficient, riding a bike will give the longer-term benefit of exercise and some mental space for restoration. Each step toward speed and efficiency comes with a cost that needs to be assessed. Philosopher Dallas Willard famously told pastor John Ortberg that he must "ruthlessly eliminate hurry" from his life in order to be spiritually healthy.[2] If our goal is to become efficient, to move faster, and to get more done, we may be cultivating a mentality that is training us in the exact opposite direction of spiritual health.

That isn't to say that efficiency is necessarily always wrong or bad for us. Rather, we fail to see the downside or costs of adopting more efficient means, such as smartphones or social media, to do things faster, with less stuff to carry around (like calendars or maps), and in less time. We also presumably can do things "better," but that drives us right to the heart of the matter. Are efficiency and increased speed always better? As is the case with traveling by car, the faster we move, the more likely we are to crash—and the more destructive the crash will be.

As noted earlier, psychologist Sherry Turkle has studied the changes brought by smartphones since their advent. After conducting extensive interviews with teenage smartphone users in the early part of this century, she found that many could not resist checking their phones while having a conversation, even if they recognized that doing so would be rude. For devices and apps that promised to make us more connected, more efficient, and more practical, they had trained teens to take actions that weakened relationships and missed important connections that were right in front of them—a very inefficient thing to do! In fact, smartphones and apps have created an expectation for constant stimulation. Turkle writes, "We enjoy continual connection but rarely have each other's full attention. We can have instant audiences but flatten out what we say to each other in new reductive genres of abbreviation. . . . New encounters need not be better to get our attention. We are wired to respond positively to their simply being new."[3]

A study from the University of Pennsylvania isolated a causal link between social media and loneliness and depression. The study included young adults ages eighteen to twenty-two and monitored their use of Facebook, Snapchat, and Instagram. For three weeks the control group maintained normal usage, while the experimental group limited themselves to ten minutes per platform each day. After evaluating screenshots of app usage and assessing the impact on fear of missing out, anxiety, depression, and loneliness, the researchers concluded, "Using less social media than you normally would leads to significant decreases in both depression and loneliness. These effects are particularly pronounced for folks who were more depressed when they came into the study."[4] The study concluded with the following assessment: "It is ironic, but perhaps not surprising, that reducing social media, which promised to help us connect with others, actually helps people feel less lonely and depressed."[5]

The nature of our usage is a major factor, since social media mixes the good with the bad. Social media use is not a single stand-alone predictor for loneliness, but it can exacerbate the bad things quickly and it doesn't solve as many problems as we expect.[6] In addition, the quality of social media use tied in with a particular goal may have a lot to do with how we feel after using it. For instance, "in a survey exploring the social media patterns of 1,781 young adults, individuals who logged in for a half an hour per day felt less lonely compared to individuals who logged on for more than two hours daily. Further, participants who logged in nine times weekly felt less isolated when compared to respondents who checked over 50 times per week."[7]

Is it possible that those who log in more often are also seeking to make connections in ways that simply aren't possible, while those using it less frequently have stronger in-person ties and see less of a need for social media in their lives? In addition, while social media may be useful for accessing information, such as the time, date, and location of events around town, it may also exacerbate a sense of missing out, personal inadequacy, and distance from others. A few posts that receive little engagement may prove dispiriting or a private message that goes unanswered may be devastating for those already feeling the crush of loneliness.

While I can certainly get the "attention" of more people at one time on social media or make immediate connections via my smartphone on the go anytime, such an efficient power comes with many inherent flaws. When posting on social media, I'm rarely getting anyone's full attention. My post is just one of the hundreds (if not thousands) of profile updates that others may scan in a given day—if the algorithm shows my post in the first place. While I'm making a weak connection with some people, especially if they leave a comment or a reply, I can make myself believe that these weak connections are actually a substantial interaction that's part of a relationship marked by presence, empathy, and emotional investment.

We don't have to look far on social media to find people with sparkling homes (who usually try to sell us cleaning products), parents with perfectly behaved children (and who are promoting an exclusive online parenting community that we can pay to join), or experts who have figured out all the problems we can't solve (who also happen to be selling online courses loaded with bonus content at an *incredible* value). The more time we spend on social media, the more likely we will feel inadequate, isolated, and alone, missing out on the fun that others are having.[8] *Fomo*

Digital technology can make certain tasks faster and more efficient, but without awareness, limits, and intention, the harmful aspects of smartphones and social media can prove too great a cost—especially when mental health issues are taken into account. Former Google employee Tristan Harris writes, "Millions of us fiercely defend our right to make 'free' choices, while we ignore how our choices are manipulated upstream by menus we didn't choose in the first place."[9] Our capacity to focus, our ability to be alone with our thoughts, and our identities are all at the mercy of our screens that are peppered with posts and notifications. This habit of stimulation, interaction, and interruption is limiting our ability to be fully present for others and for spiritual practices, but there are also issues that spill into our social connections. Society itself is being shaped, or fragmented, by digital technology and social media. As bad as this may seem, even if we're not done considering the bad news, all is not lost. Christianity has the deep roots of tradition and the spiritual practices that can help us respond in constructive ways to the fragmentation and distraction fostered by social media. Hang in there. We will get to some solutions soon enough. However, we first need to get a better handle on the ways social media and digital devices are changing society.

THE DIGITAL FORMATION OF SOCIETY

In 2013, Justine Sacco boarded a flight to South Africa as the senior director of corporate communications at the Internet brand company IAC. By the time she set foot at her destination, she had become the target of social media outrage and had been fired from her position. How she went from a highly valued communication professional to social media pariah in less than twelve hours offers a concerning glimpse into the dark side of social media.

I remember seeing Sacco's tweet and sharing the surprise and outrage of so many others. Sacco tweeted, "Going to Africa. Hope I don't get AIDS. Just kidding. I'm white!" While the public outrage increased with every retweet and criticism of Sacco's apparent racism, someone launched a hashtag, #HasJustineLandedYet, and that helped the public spectacle of her shaming become a global phenomenon.

Shortly after her flight arrived, Sacco learned that she had been fired because of her tweet. Her coworkers were horrified at the thought of working with her; her company ran from her PR disaster; and the rest of the Internet could rest easy that a terrible racist person had been put in her place. I would suspect that some of the folks who look like me also felt a sense of relief that we wouldn't have to interrogate our own roles in addressing racism, since we're at least not as racist as Justine Sacco—she's what a real racist looks like.

However, we'd all made a significant error.

About a year after the incident, the *New York Times* followed up on Sacco's story to learn her side of things. Sacco asserted that she believed no reasonable person would take her tweet literally. She shared:

> To me it was so insane of a comment for anyone to make. . . . I thought there was no way that anyone could possibly think it was literal. . . . Unfortunately, I am not a character on 'South Park' or a comedian, so I had no business commenting on the epidemic in such a politically incorrect manner on a public platform. . . . To put it simply, I wasn't trying to raise awareness of AIDS or piss off the world or ruin my life. Living in America puts us in a bit of a bubble when it comes to what is going on in the third world. I was making fun of that bubble.[10]

With this perspective in mind, I had to consider a new explanation for her remark: Sacco thought she was making a sarcastic remark among a small circle of followers who knew her. However, the public nature of that remark opened the possibility of it being interpreted in ways Sacco claims she never intended. There is certainly a lot of room for debate about whether her intended effect even among a small circle of friends was appropriate or helpful, but Sacco had no intention of broadcasting ignorant, racist remarks to the world. Without context, facial expressions, or voice inflection to convey sarcasm, it's easy for a social media post to take on a life of its own. We can easily forget about the humanity of others involved, reacting only to what we see and often following the cues of others rather than asking for more context or insight.

Adding to our challenges as a society, bad news travels much faster and sticks in our minds much better than good news on social media. Fear and polarization can take hold easily, sowing division and discord among groups that would otherwise find ways to coexist without suspicion of the other. According to its creators, social media is supposed to bring people together. For a time, it looked like it might even work on impossibly large scales: democracy activists used social media in the early 2010s to organize the Arab Spring protests calling for democratic governments in places such as Tunisia, Libya, Egypt, and Syria. However, social media analysts believe that groups quickly polarized and divided as social media created the perfect storm for political division and chaos. One study concluded:

> Social media challenges democratic consolidation by accelerating and intensifying dangerous trends such as polarization, fear and dehumanization of rivals. The speed, emotional intensity and echo-chamber qualities of social media content make those exposed to it experience more extreme reactions. Social media is particularly suited to worsening political and social polarization because of its ability to spread violent images and frightening rumors extremely quickly and intensely through relatively closed communities of the like-minded.[11]

Once enough people react publicly to an event, it's hard to take a careful step backward for reconsideration. While social media influencers "win" the attention battle by being the first to report on or respond to a jarring or emotionally charged story, that can put the truth in the back seat. Clicks, shares, and other measures of engagement can begin to matter more

Wow!

Wow!

than whether an event happened, or whether our analysis is correct. P. W. Singer and Emerson Brooking argue in *LikeWar: The Weaponization of Social Media* that on social media, "Fact is a matter of consensus. Eliminate that consensus, and fact becomes a matter of opinion. Learn how to command and manipulate that opinion, and you are entitled to reshape the fabric of the world."[12] While the average social media user isn't fabricating news stories or trying to gain influence through posting divisive content, we are all exposed to this divisive and fragmented ecosystem. We may even become deceived or worried by some of this content. Users who go on social media to share about their family or to read the insights from experts could end up angry about an ignorant statement, distracted by a quirky video, or concerned about a politician's policies before fully grasping the complexities, implications, or basic facts of a situation.

Social media isn't designed to promote the most accurate or the most carefully assembled information. On social media, a study that offers a careful, measured assessment of its findings will always lose out to the emotionally charged spin-off article from a partisan site that twists the study's findings to confirm the suspicions and bias of readers—thus ensuring that the average person is more likely to miss the original study. There is no denying that we want to find the inside edge on information or the story that is being suppressed by the establishment because we feel like we're part of something special and significant. I have often had to reckon with that feeling in my own evaluation of news stories on social media. Once a compelling narrative engages our emotions, it's hard to shut down the desire to be the first to share it and to win the respect and attention of our social media followers. One former Facebook executive,

Chamath Palihapitiya, framed this matter in stark terms: "The short-term, dopamine-driven feedback loops that we have created are destroying how society works. No civil discourse, no cooperation; misinformation, mistruth. . . . This is a global problem. It is eroding the core foundations of how people behave by and between each other."[13]

This isn't to say that social media is the sole cause of social division. Rather, it makes division more likely because of the way it rewards certain inflammatory behaviors and emotionally charged accusations. As we are tossed about in the highs and lows of social media today, we would all benefit from a careful assessment of its downside and why so many of its creators, engineers, and executives are warning us about its dangers. In fact, if social media and digital devices were so good for us, we would expect the innovators behind these tools to immerse their children in these devices designed to make the world more "connected." The reality may surprise you . . . or given the ground we've covered so far, it may not.

HIGH-TECH LEADERS AND THEIR LOW-TECH KIDS

If saturating our society with digital devices and social media access is going to make our world a better, more connected place with all kinds of benefits for education, information, and networking, then we would expect technology leaders to immerse their children in their products and to pioneer the use of their apps. We would expect the children of every Apple employee to have an iPad, and we would surely expect these parents to immerse their children's schools in the very best, most cutting-edge technology available. The technology giants have sold computers, iPads, and other devices at a discount to schools for years. If the companies are willing to pass up some profit for the sake of educating children across the country, then surely their employees would want the same technological advantages and benefits for their children, right? Would the people who got ahead because of digital technology risk leaving their children behind in an economy that relies on technological innovation?

On the contrary, many of the people who design our technology and social media keep their children far from it or severely limit their access. Apple cofounder Steve Jobs famously said in an interview that his kids didn't use an iPad and that technology was very limited in his home.[14] Microsoft founder Bill Gates likewise instituted strict technology use boundaries with his children. Several of the private schools serving many children of leading technology innovators are completely free of technology for children under eleven years old.[15]

Does that send up any red flags for you?

Wouldn't the creators of digital devices expect their children to be the most important endorsement of all for the benefits of their products? Can you imagine taking your children to a restaurant where the chefs would never feed their own families or an amusement park where none of the employees would let their children on the rides?

As it turns out, the leaders of technology companies are being extremely prudent in their parenting and schooling decisions. Former Facebook vice president for user growth Chamath Palihapitiya has some strong thoughts on how Facebook is harming society and how he handles it with his children: "I can control my decision, which is that I don't use that s***. I can control my kids' decisions, which is that they're not allowed to use that s***."[16] Palihapitiya's strong response is no doubt based in part on the mental health statistics related to younger social media users. Depression, anxiety, and suicide rates among teens and young adults bumped up noticeably once smart-phones, tablets, and social media began to be integrated into childhood.[17]

The Independent reported the following technology trends among children: "Research has found that an eighth-grader's risk for depression jumps 27% when he or she frequently uses so-cial media. Kids who use their phones for at least three hours a day are much more likely to be suicidal. And recent research has found the teen suicide rate in the US now eclipses the homicide rate, with smartphones as the driving force."[18] No one is arguing against the right of a company to meet consumer need and to make a profit from it. My contention is that technology and social media companies are having a profoundly negative impact on human flourishing, and that they fully know it, protect their children from it, and yet continue to develop features to make their products difficult to resist and almost compulsive to use, regardless of the harm done to their customers.

The warnings from mental health professionals, coupled with the actions of social media executives and whistleblowers like Tristan Harris, Ellen Pao, and Palihapitiya, should give us pause. Speaking most optimistically, social media and digital device companies are not spending enough time considering the damage of their products on users, given that they treat their children's technology use far differently than that of their customers. In the worst-case scenario, they have chosen profit over the well-being of society.

As of this writing, social media and technology companies have not responded in a cohesive or hopeful manner to these charges about their products—although small changes have been made, such as the Screen Time feature on iPhones that offers a weekly report on app use and the time spent on the phone in general. Considering that many whistleblowers are coming from the ranks of tech companies, we're hardly dealing with conspiracy theories or individuals leveraging false accusations for the sake of publicity or getting a payday from a trumped-up lawsuit settlement. These are serious charges that can dramatically affect our mental, physical, and spiritual well-being.

Beyond the design and intent of social media apps and digital devices, there is another factor: content. Specifically, some makers of content, from articles to videos to images to tweets, know how social media is designed to work and how it's changing society. They are playing the system to reach their goals regardless of the influence it has on individuals or society. Our concern isn't just with the design of social media apps themselves. We also need to become aware of the content that we consume on social media each day—specifically where it's coming from and the goals of its creators.

SOCIAL MEDIA NEWS GIVES US THE BLUES

Anxiety became my regular struggle in the year after the 2016 U.S. election. Time and time again, I returned to the stress of social media and the ongoing commentary on the news it offered. As I sought out the opinions of experts on social media, I inevitably exposed myself to despairing, angry, or combative commentary that sent my anxiety through the roof. As each new crisis appeared to unfold, I engaged further with the news and experts to find out what was going on. Over time, this exposure to conflict and despair took its toll, and I found myself needing to limit my exposure to social media, to say nothing of spending less time on my phone. Each week I set new boundaries around my social media use, noticing how raw emotions of fear, outrage, and despair sometimes shifted according to what I saw on my screen.

This cycle of outrage and fear is the kind of thing that I couldn't quite put my finger on as a one-time event or news story. Rather, I traced my stress, fear, or anxiety to accessing news and troubling trends in current events through the social media ecosystem. Consider this: Across the board, psychologists reported a dramatic increase in stress and anxiety after the 2016 election,[19] and the future of the nation was a significant source of stress for 63 percent of Americans in a 2017 survey.[20] This wasn't just among immigrants, people of color, or Muslims, all of whom were targeted by alarming policy shifts and extremist groups who became a far more visible part of the political right. This increase in anxiety and depression also occurred among white people who weren't directly targeted by many of the concerning policies. It certainly didn't help that news executives were incentivized to push the most disturbing and fearful stories, since their ratings increased as anxiety over the news skyrocketed. One executive at CBS shared the following about covering the divisive 2016 election: "It may not be good for America, but it's d*** good for CBS."[21]

Where was this anxiety, stress, and depression coming from? Arthur C. Evans Jr., chief executive officer of the American Psychological Association, offered the following conclusions based on his analysis of the APA's "Stress in America" survey: "With 24-hour news networks and conversations with friends, family and other connections on social media, it's hard to avoid the constant stream of stress around issues of national concern. . . . Understanding that we all still need to be informed about the news, it's time to make it a priority to be thoughtful about how often and what type of media we consume."[22] We could say, "The news cycle is responsible," leave it there, and probably get the picture partly correct. However, we're consuming news content throughout the day on our smartphones and on social media, and we might also consider that this form of access and interaction with news may leave us more worried and distracted. In other words, it's not just the news but how the news is presented and how it is consumed on social media and omnipresent smartphones.

As of 2018, 47 percent of Americans relied on social media as a convenient way to access news, with only 21 percent hardly ever accessing social media for news. While television remained the top source of news, as of 2018, 20 percent of Americans used social media as their primary news source, which was only 6 percent behind radio news (26 percent) and 4 percent higher than newspapers (16 percent).[23] Relying on social media for either the sourcing of news or commentary on news immediately injects large numbers of reactions to each story. In addition, social media users should be highly critical of the reliability of the news outlets sharing articles on social media. In fact, the fake news stories shared on social media by creators with the intention of making a quick buck, sowing division, or smearing someone's reputation travel significantly faster and wider than true news stories.[24] Adding to the complexity of social media's impact, a lot of the content being promoted and shared can be traced to automated "bots," programs designed to post specific content as if they were real people. For instance, in a study of tweets during a period in 2017, 66 percent of the content shared on Twitter was linked to bots[25]; another study estimated that 9–15 percent of the accounts on Twitter were bots, programmed to influence what trends each day.[26]

Even if we don't believe that bots or trolls are changing how we read and interact with news on social media, social media is still a challenging place to interact with news stories. Suppose for a moment that we visit social media and see a link to a credible news story that may be concerning, but the person sharing it offers a doomsday commentary. This person may have no expertise on the topic at hand, yet the reaction itself, highlighted with an alarming red siren emoji, may punch us in the gut and trigger an emotional response. In fact, several others may follow up by commenting with comparable gloom and desperation. It is quite likely that these responses don't match the true stakes in the news story, but will we even read beyond the headline and seek other experienced perspectives to help us put the story in context? This is before we even ask whether the news story itself is credible, well-sourced, and accurate in its analysis. Have we considered other points of view? Once we sense the threat of this story, we may spend the rest of the afternoon with a sense of panic and unease.

In another scenario, we may visit social media sites and see several friends reacting to a news story about a pastor's divisive comments. These are credible, trustworthy people whom we believe to be sensible and discerning. However, today they are angry about a sensational report they've just read on a news site you've never heard of. Several friends share this story, and it includes quotes and reactions from the main actors involved in the disturbing comments. Perhaps their responses are warranted? However, the more you review the website, which uses an official-sounding newspaper title with a word like *Post* or *Courier* in it, the more questions you have. The quotes shared from the pastor are short, and are not even complete sentences in most cases. Even more concerning, no other major news outlet has reported on this pastor's comments. Should you trust this sensational site even though every person in this story has acted in ways that you find believable, if not how you expected? Once anger, fear, or anxiety has been triggered through an interaction on social media, we may have a fight-or-flight reaction. Suddenly, because we are angry, fearful, or anxious, all we can see is a threat—regardless of the story's credibility or the expertise of the various accounts reacting to it.

It's difficult to face how effectively social media manipulates our emotions and our analysis of news. When pairing social media with a concerted campaign to persuade people in their thinking, it is the ideal tool for injecting emotionally charged videos and images to persuade people, to sow doubt, or to encourage despair. We are most vulnerable when we believe that we are too savvy or sophisticated to avoid this manipulation. Thomas Merton recognized that in a democratic society, especially one where so many of the poor and vulnerable have a great deal on the line, voting citizens needed to be thoughtful and well-informed. He worried that mass media in the 1960s had already become a kind of affliction that prevented deep thought and clear decisions. If automatic reactions are a threat to the stability of society, then social media may be one of the most potent tools around for sowing outrage, despair, and plenty of other negative emotions. Adding the power of social media to our partisan political and media climate has fulfilled Merton's concerns about politics and media:

> Action is not governed by moral reason but by political expediency and the demands of technology—translated into the simple abstract formulas of propaganda. These formulas have nothing to do with reasoned moral action, even though they

may appeal to apparent moral values—they simply condition the mass of men to react in a desired way to certain stimuli.

Men do not agree in moral reasoning. They concur in the emotional use of slogans and political formulas. There is no persuasion but that of power, of quantity, of pressure, of fear, of desire. Such is our present condition—and it is critical![27]

The negative results of social media up to this point in history have been tribalization, manipulation, and the amplification of emotionally stirring stories that may or may not be true. If the past ten years are any indication of what's coming in the future, that push to extremes may only grow worse as technology opens new possibilities for manipulating videos and news stories.

FAKE NEWS AND MISINFORMATION

If social media thrives in the crucible of strong emotions, compelling narratives, and extreme viewpoints, then we shouldn't be surprised that they have become information warfare and propaganda battlefields. While many of us adopted social media in order to learn more about what's going on with our friends, to connect with our family, and to share updates from our lives, these networks are now polluted with deceptive stories and sophisticated, highly compelling disinformation campaigns. Moving forward, there is one assumption that will serve us well: we have all been deceived at some point on social media.

We need to make this assumption because it is most likely true for all of us, and it will help us face the complexity of this issue that will call for wisdom, humility, and compassion. Even as we face the truth about the deceptive stories and profiles on social media, we should never think that we are somehow above the reactions of the masses. There's an art to crafting viral social media content, a dark art especially for the purveyors of made-up news stories. P. W. Singer and Emerson Brooking, the authors of *LikeWar*, suggest that social media content thrives if it can fuse together the following elements: narrative, emotion, authenticity, community, and inundation.[28] The narrative must be simple. In fact, politicians are using simpler vocabulary and slogans because they travel particularly well in the social media environment.[29] When the goal is stimulation, emotion, and a particular action or inaction, substance isn't necessary. However, these deceptive campaigns are sophisticated, and they target both sides of the political spectrum, pushing them to their extremes. At times they may appear small in scale, but we shouldn't overlook their cumulative effect. Technology pioneer and now social media critic Jaron Lanier argues the following:

> It's important to understand the nature of the problem. The effects of social media manipulation are slight at any given time. But slight changes applied consistently and carefully can have big effects. An initially minute compound interest can turn into a big reward for a patient investor. In the same way, slight but predictable changes to the behavior of a population can be gained through adaptive algorithmic adjustments to social media expectations.[30]

We are all quite likely to fall for deceptive information campaigns or to fruitlessly engage with divisive trolls at one point or another. I've even unintentionally interacted with them.

My social media mentions are generally low on drama. While I'm certainly committed to posting primarily about removing our obstacles to prayer, I sometimes wade into the justice and equality issues of the day, aiming to provide a constructive Christian perspective (but you win some and you lose some). However, a number of Twitter users replied to me with anger, outrage, personal insults, and unhinged comments when I waded into online discussions about immigration, the evangelical advisers to the president, and the plans of the vice president to speak at my alma mater's graduation ceremony.

The change was stark and noticeable. Suddenly, people showed up to insult me, to accuse me of self-promotion, and to dismiss the idiocy of my comments. Some commenters linked to images and "news stories" that allegedly proved that violent gangs were pouring over the borders of America or that religious freedom in America was hanging on by a thread. The profiles of these accounts, if they even had any pictures or information, appeared to focus only on politics. Many had long strings of random numbers as their Twitter handles and American flag emojis. At first I just assumed some people had odd ways of setting up their social media accounts. However, as I learned more about bots that are programmed to target specific trends and trolls who only attack their opponents on social media, I realized that I had been targeted by some combination of bots and trolls who sought to silence and minimize my views. In reacting and replying to them, I had been taken in by one of the many deceptions on social media.

Why do fake stories, fake accounts, and misinformation work? It's often because we react to the headline or the reply without considering the profile in question, carefully reading the inflammatory story, or comparing the story with other credible sources. Once our emotions are triggered, we are ready to take action. To my surprise, I still haven't won an argument with a computer program.

Most importantly, it's shockingly easy to uncritically accept what we find on social media. This is a major factor when it comes to fabricated news stories and the accounts that push them, even if scrutiny reveals that those accounts are obviously bots or trolls. Confirmation bias is a powerful force online, as "we're more likely to notice stories of acts that fit what we already believe (or want to believe)."[31] If we're already inclined to react in a certain way, we may well be naturally drawn to news stories that back up our conclusions rather than call them into question.

Researchers at the Massachusetts Institute of Technology found that throughout the life cycle of 126,000 tweets that were rigorously fact-checked, the false stories spread about six times faster than the true stories.[32] During the 2016 U.S. election season there were literally thousands of accounts churning out millions of fake social posts in service of a variety of agendas.[33] Fake stories actually dominated on Facebook in the three months leading up to the 2016 election, and a study of 22 million tweets found that real news stories couldn't compete with the number of shares of misinformation, polarizing stories, and conspiracy-fueled conjectures.[34]

Even more disturbing is the finding from a Stanford study that more than 80 percent of middle school students couldn't determine the difference between an ad and a news story. Meanwhile, most high school students struggled to discern whether manipulated images were genuine, were unlikely to click through a link to evaluate a source's credibility, and even when comparing the credibility of organizations, often struggled to figure out which was more reliable.[35] Students immersed in social media aren't prepared for the onslaught of deception and misinformation that could very likely leave them worried, angry, or deceived. It is not hard to have these fabricated news stories in view while reading Merton's words:

> Democracy cannot exist when men prefer ideas and opinions that are fabricated for them. The actions and statements of the citizen must not be mere automatic "reactions"—mere mechanical salutes, gesticulations signifying passive conformity with the dictates of those in power.
>
> To be truthful, we will have to admit that one cannot expect this to be realized in all citizens of a democracy. But if it is not realized in a significant proportion of them, democracy ceases to be an objective fact and becomes nothing but an emotionally loaded word.[36]

Whether those stories are fabricated by someone looking to make a quick buck[37] or by a hostile nation, fake news is often designed to either rally people to anger or sow despair.

I have most certainly been manipulated and deceived by social media. This may have resulted in despair, outrage, or a few extra shares. It can be humiliating, infuriating, and angering to find out that you've been "fooled" on social media. However, it's a mistake to believe that only "fools" are fooled. We are dealing with highly sophisticated campaigns that are targeting our preexisting fears and desires. We shouldn't be surprised that we have all likely fallen for some form of misinformation or manipulation.

If we are going to recover from the deception, fear, and division that has flooded our digital devices and apps, we need genuine grace for others and humility for our own limitations. In fact, the image of a "flood" of information, good, bad, or distracting, offers a helpful ending point for our look at the impact of social media on individuals and on society.

INFORMATION OVERLOAD

While the Internet started with the promise of wide access to all the information in the world and an equal platform for all ideas to thrive, it has also created a perfect storm of information overload. Writing in the 1960s, Merton knew about newspapers, magazines, books, the radio, and a few television stations and concluded, "The greatest need of our time is to clean out the enormous mass of mental and emotional rubbish that clutters our minds and makes of all political and social life a mass illness. Without this housecleaning we cannot begin to see. Unless we see we cannot think."[38]

We now have twenty-four-hour news, the never-ending deluge of social media updates, and a steady stream of email that we unleash if we sign up for enough websites. The infinite scrolling feature on most social media sites makes it possible to always find something else, and there will always be a big, bold BREAKING NEWS headline on news websites demanding our attention. Back in the early 1980s, philosopher Jacques Ellul noted that a deluge of information had already resulted in people struggling to determine what was relevant to them and making the error of choosing sources according to personal preference: "The point that always seems the most important is that the individual is becoming incapable not only of differentiating between true and false information, but differentiating between the information which has a real effect on his life and that which is irrelevant. The enormous quantity of information . . . There is not time to read it."[39]

Thanks to this far-reaching access to online content, we can always find something to be happy about, something to be sad about, and something to be angry about. Disasters and injustices around the world are available for us around the clock, and it doesn't take long to experience despair and to desire an escape from the suffering in the world. While the equal access of the Internet for everyone brings many benefits, sifting through the deluge of information and disinformation is quite another matter. We can wear ourselves out by immersing ourselves in the suffering of others or nurturing our anger over the injustices of our time. That isn't to say that the solution is "ignorance is bliss." That is hardly the point! Rather, we must find a way to remain aware of and engaged with the people around us and informed about the important issues of our times without losing our grounding and stability in God's presence. This brings up a vital distinction that is often lost in our time of information overload and emotional reactions on social media to the twenty-four-hour news cycle. Is remaining emotionally enraged and constantly aware inspiring us toward meaningful action that could lead to human flourishing and the benefit of our neighbors?

Most importantly, there are groups and resources that can help us remain engaged in the issues of our time, aware of current events, and directed toward meaningful action rather than impotent rage. After the 2016 election, I struggled to channel my roller coaster of emotions in a positive direction. Most days I struggled to even think straight as the deluge of bad news sent my mind spinning. I wasn't much help for anyone, let alone myself and my family. As my wife and I discussed what to do, we settled on supporting a few groups who addressed justice and equality among the vulnerable. I also became more involved in serving at our church, which is well connected to many of the social service agencies in our town. Some days, with talk of war and climate change topping my list of stress sources, these steps felt like tossing pebbles at a raging tsunami.

However, I could function better each day rather than bearing the crippling weight of despair and anxiety. I was beginning to disconnect from the despair and rage machine of social media so I could reconnect with the people in my community and organizations dedicated to meeting the specific needs of our time and place.

One professor found himself in a similar situation, and he engaged in a full-on blackout of news and social media for an entire year. He and a friend also found a measure of hope and direction by supporting groups that were engaged in the issues he judged most pressing. Most notably, he managed to maintain a wider perspective of events rather than being immobilized by the highs and lows of the daily news cycle. He noted after his experiment, "Getting depressed. Yelling at the TV. Complaining with friends. Tweeting about how mad we are. We spend so much time consuming news . . . that we don't have any energy or emotion left to do anything about it."[40] Each person will require different boundaries according to their mental and emotional needs. My concern is that we can be immobilized by the ongoing deluge of rage, anxiety, and fear that streams toward us each day through social media and our smartphones. It's hard enough to process the news each day without a caption along the lines of "Goodbye, Democracy!"

Stepping back for a moment to review the terrain we've covered, we've seen that social media and digital devices are designed to be extremely engaging, compulsive, and even addicting, in the sense of behavior addiction. Social media is designed to reward content that drives engagement, but it ends up rewarding the most combative and divisive content. Social media companies value engagement over all else and have no incentive to remove fake news or potentially harmful content. Psychologists and researchers have found links to deteriorating well-being and mental health among those with increased usage of social media.

Digital technology is training users to expect quick hits of connection, engagement, and affirmation, limiting the ability of users to focus on in-person interactions. While most users report increased distraction thanks to their phones and social media, the impact goes far beyond that for individuals and society. For Christians, social media and digital devices are capable of profoundly harming our spiritual health, especially how we spend our time, what we think about, and where we derive our identity from. Now that we have a handle on digital technology's wider impact on individuals and society, let's consider how this specifically shows up in the practices of Christian spirituality.

... INVITATION TO RECONNECT ....

Consider your reasons for using a smartphone or other digital devices. Then consider how you spend time with them each day. Do your intentions match your current usage?

Take note today of how social media affects your mood or emotions. Is there a particular story or comment that you found especially distressing?

Consider the most negative interaction and most positive interaction you've had in the comments on social media. How can they inform your future use?

It seems that our remedies are instinctively those which aggravate the sickness: the remedies are expressions of the sickness itself.

—THOMAS MERTON

THREE

How Digital Formation Hinders Spirituality

In her extensive interviews with teenagers, Sherry Turkle found that for youth, setting up their first social media profiles had become a rite of passage. Many also described it as a moment of profound crisis. The pressure to present a suitable image of themselves in their profile pictures and an engaging description of themselves, coupled with the fear of rejection or mockery, demolished the joy of interacting with their friends online. Even for those generally unworried about the response of peers, social media still prompts us to curate our identity, selecting the "best" parts of ourselves to share with others. This sets a perfect trap of sorts in terms of spirituality, as we already have more than enough opportunities to present or live under the influence of a fabricated false self.

When I speak of a false self, I mean that kind of mask or identity we imagine for ourselves. Henri Nouwen served in both ministry and the academic world and frequently brushed up against the image he hoped to project about himself. He wrote in *The Way of the Heart* about the pressure in ministry to be relevant and competent, rather than embracing the brokenness we find in silence and solitude.[1] Brennan Manning famously called the false self "the imposter" in his book *Abba's Child*, implying that the false self steals something our true selves should be receiving. Whether we try to project ourselves as successful, organized, creative, wise, or smart, the false self steals the security and affirmation we could receive from God. Instead, we are pressured to maintain and even protect the false self rather than discovering who we are in God.

Social media provides an opportunity to make the false self more concrete—at least in the sense that it becomes something you and others can see. It literally can become an avatar that is projected, and as we become entangled with our online personas and false selves, it may become quite difficult to discern who we are in the security of God's love. As more likes and followers amass in approval of the false self, we may fear the loss of this steady stream of affirmation and may do what we can to ensure that it continues to grow. This isn't to say that every social media user is at the mercy of a false self. Rather, social media offers a perfect opportunity to "incarnate" the false self and to build relationships around it.

Even if we manage to share a relatively authentic version of ourselves and have an inner grounding in the love and acceptance of God, that doesn't mean our connections with others will be authentic or deep on social media. We can only interact at the levels we reveal. Turkle writes, "Social media asks us to represent ourselves in simplified ways. And then, faced with an audience, we feel pressure to conform to these simplifications."[2] Many of the students whom Turkle interviewed admitted that they spent significant time crafting a profile that felt phony, knew many of their friends had done the same, and performed for their friends in order to get the affirmation of "likes" on social media.[3] The consequences of tarnishing one's image, whether in real life or on social media, can be especially harrowing for teens using social media. Instagram, for one, has become a platform for some of the worst online bullying for image-conscious teens.[4]

Are we truly seeing people as they are? Or are we only seeing a projected image that is meant to appeal to us? Thomas Merton noted this interpersonal tension with love when he wrote, "The beginning of love is the will to let those we love be perfectly themselves, the resolution not to twist them to fit our own image. If in loving them we do not love what they are, but only their potential likeness to ourselves, then we do not love them: we only love the reflection of ourselves we find in them."[5] As algorithms help us find people who are most like ourselves and as social media results in people migrating toward divided echo chambers, we are at risk of losing touch with the complexity of each other while also reducing people to simplistic labels based on what they reveal online about themselves, such as their religious or political preferences.

While there are opportunities for connection, community, and encouragement via social media notifications, those notifications can also serve as a source of insecurity that drives us back to social media for another hit of affirmation. (By the way, you can easily turn them off under your phone's settings—click on "Notifications" to customize which apps can send them to you.) This ready-made, daily affirmation from friends, family, and even complete strangers can make it difficult, if not impossible, to give up a social media affirmation hub like Instagram or Twitter—although services like Facebook, YouTube, and Snapchat offer many similar quandaries for users seeking affirmation. You could get "amazing feedback" at any moment if you keep checking, keep posting, and then keep checking. This feedback loop runs counter to the vision for contentment offered by Merton:

> In order to settle down in the quiet of our own being we must learn to be detached from the results of our own activity. We must withdraw ourselves, to some extent, from the effects that are beyond our control and be content with the good will and the work that are the quiet expression of our inner life. We must be content to live without watching ourselves live, to work without expecting any immediate reward, to love without an instantaneous satisfaction, and to exist without any special recognition.[6]

The feedback on social media is quite immediate, especially if you compare it to older publishing processes, such as a magazine article. We immediately know if our ideas, images, videos, or favorite articles resonate with our family, friends, and colleagues. The elation of that feedback can become addicting. At the same time, we can also enjoy reading updates, viewing videos, and browsing photos from our friends, which go on in an endless supply. We have no end of sources for comparison and envy. The more we fill our days with the parade of images and videos on social media, the less likely we are to turn to God for our affirmation, identity, and security.

If social media creates a crisis of identity, it can also create a crisis of emotion. As we view the content that is most "engaging" and most likely to generate a response, we run the risk of living in a constant state of reaction and interaction. Our minds can become full of thoughts, making it quite difficult to pray as we process the latest enraging news story or a frustrating interaction on social media.

TOO REACTIVE TO RECEIVE

Two contemporary teachers of contemplative prayer offer us two helpful, but quite different, pictures of what it looks like to pray today. Both pictures will help us consider the influence of thoughts and emotions in our attempts to be present and aware of God.

Martin Laird writes about the movement of our thoughts from reactive mind to receptive mind to the peaceful aware-ness of God with what he calls luminous mind. Many of us begin praying in a state of reactive mind. When I have been engaged in social media, especially after replying to combative comments, I have very much felt the burden of reactive mind as I process ideas, struggle with anger or disappointment, and an-alyze my overanalyzing. Laird suggests that reactive mind feels a bit like being trapped in a phone booth with a bee. We feel agitated, fearful, and on high alert, reacting in the moment to the perceived threat before us. Perhaps the good news is that the bee is easily avoided if we know how to depart from the phone booth and disengage from our thoughts. Nevertheless, if we carry social media with us on our smartphones and oth-er devices wherever we go, our reactive minds will have no shortage of material to work with since we have locked our-selves in the reactionary phone booth—and unlike a certain police call box, this booth is not bigger on the inside. We'll remain in the phone booth, swatting furiously and never seeing the emptiness of these thoughts. In relation to the false self,

Laird notes that those who leave behind reactive mind are also leaving the thoughts bouncing around that are "generating story upon story to such an extent that we derived a sense of identity from our tightly-wound world of thoughts. Or . . . we derived a sense of identity based on what we thought others must be thinking of us."[7]

Reactive mind is also restless, fully given over to the compulsions of our image-conscious consumer culture. Laird describes reactive mind as a compulsion to acquire and to make progress toward mastery. "It is . . . shaped by a culture that feeds on compulsion, consumption, conquest, credit, and cash," he writes. "There is a frightened, defensive quality to reactive mind that is always at the ready. It is second nature to us and supported by a heavy momentum that has been generated by a lifetime of going through life merely reacting to what is going on with us and around us."[8]

If Laird's bee in the phone booth is too distressing, or if you don't know what a phone booth is (trust me, they were terrible . . . unless you were Superman), perhaps Thomas Keating can help with a different picture that illustrates the challenges of prayer. Keating suggests that our thoughts come to mind like an endless series of boats floating down a stream. We can choose to remain grounded in the present moment, waiting patiently on God as we meditate on Scripture or pray in silence. We can also choose to hop on a boat and take that thought for a ride downstream. Who knows what kind of turbulence awaits us downstream, and surely some thoughts will be less stable than others as the currents swirl and shift.

The spiritual teachers of the church have historically taken steps to minimize their distractions and thoughts. The desert fathers and mothers moved to the wilderness outside Alexandria,

Egypt, and the wilderness outside Jerusalem to escape the controversies and concerns of the cities. They practiced simple prayers while working or in larger gatherings. Whether they were hermits or community members who practiced regular solitude, they welcomed visitors and offered instruction to the area churches drawn from the wisdom they developed from their dedicated time in solitude. Routine time with the clarity of thought that came from being disentangled from the daily stream of thoughts gave them wisdom and clarity that the people of their time highly valued. The more they withdrew from the daily flow of information, the more stability they found.

The anonymous Carthusian writer of *The Cloud of Unknowing* offered novices a rather militant approach to distracting thoughts at the outset of his manual for prayer, suggesting that they more or less fight off distracting thoughts with a relentless prayer word. Martin Laird notes that this combative approach may not prove helpful for all people at all times, but it can be especially useful for those starting out spiritual practices and who find themselves immersed in afflictive thoughts. We could say that this is a kind of detoxing process that can become less jarring as we settle into the simplicity of returning to our intention to be present for God and letting thoughts go with a simple prayer word, such as *beloved*.[9]

The ability to access social media, podcasts, news, text messages, games, and articles anytime on our smartphones means that we never have to be alone with our thoughts. We are trained to crave stimulation, the little dopamine hit of affirmation from a notification or new email. There's always a breaking story to consider or a hot take on that story to react against. The more immersed we are in news, social media interactions, and other forms of media on our smartphones that can travel anywhere, the more crammed our minds become. This can make us far more reactive, unaware of the thoughts taking up residence in our minds. As these thoughts accumulate, our ability to sort through them is diminished, and our default can become a kind of reactive stance. Rather than carefully sorting through them and their impact on us, we can fall into a pattern of more or less swatting at a bee or frantically jumping from boat to boat.

At the root here is how technology hinders our freedom to think clearly. While we are free to immerse ourselves in information, somewhere along the way we can lose our self-awareness and grounding. Merton wrote about the impact of this on our spiritual receptivity: "Man cannot assent to a spiritual message as long as his mind and heart are enslaved by automatism. He will always remain so enslaved as long as he is submerged in a mass of other automatons, without individuality and without their rightful integrity as persons."[10]

Losing time for a quiet mind, to say nothing of solitude and silence, makes us more likely to be reactive and unable to process the thoughts in our minds. Our cluttered minds won't have much space left for prayer, meditation on Scripture, or other spiritual practices that could ground us in our true identity in God. In fact, the reactive, overwhelming nature of social media and smartphones doesn't just affect our own inner states. This reactive state also affects how we interact with one another.

UNITED IN DIVISION

If there's one thing Christians can agree on about social media, it's that we aren't as bad as those "other" Christians who post things opposed to the teaching of Jesus—*wink, wink*. Whatever your theological background, someone who embodies the worst qualities of an opposing viewpoint likely came to mind as you read that last sentence.

Of course, as Paul noted, there will be disagreements among Christians. We can't say that everyone is right! However, we have never been more aware of those with different beliefs or actions, and that can fuel more division as we fight with each other on social media.

Social media is a terrible medium for a debate, especially about our most cherished beliefs. We tend to immediately become defensive when we have made our views public, and it can be hard to really hear others. Our mistakes could be on display for hundreds, if not thousands of social media users! We also can't reliably discern the tone of the comments we receive, let alone judge how we are coming across to others.

I have seen more than enough online controversies develop among Christian pastors and writers, but I have also made my fair share of mistakes. The one that stands out in particular is the time *Christianity Today* sent me a complimentary copy of their magazine. Someone in their marketing department must have figured that a writer like me would help promote their current issue. They literally could not have chosen a worse issue to send me. A prominent "religious liberty" advocate from the largest Protestant denomination in America graced the cover, along with a headline insinuating that he was now marginalized. I almost fell out of my chair. While a man who teaches that women can't teach or lead men will naturally end up in the cultural minority today, this was hardly a matter of a white man in a massive denomination becoming marginalized—even if the feature article qualified this as "culturally marginalized." There are plenty of Christians who live on the margins of society, but they look quite different from this man, who has extensive resources and influential contacts. I didn't see how the editorial board at *Christianity Today* could make such a bad call, and in the moment of my reaction, I dropped a hot take on social media.

As you can expect with social media, the comments and replies savaged the cover. My hot take sparked a raging inferno of insults about the agenda of the editors, the intelligence of the editors, and even their lack of creativity in word choice. As much as I disliked that cover, I immediately regretted my posting. I regretted it even more when the primary editor responsible for the cover replied to some of the comments—as it turned out, she was a friend of mine on Facebook.

My first major mistake was the assumption that the cover was the work of a team. It wasn't. It turns out that this editor, and Facebook friend, was very much involved in the cover design. While I still strongly disagreed with her, I realized that I felt justified in my public shaming of the cover because I imagined a faceless roundtable of editors who were out of touch with those who were actually suffering on the margins. The reality looked a bit more like an editor's judgment call— an incorrect one in my estimation, but still a decision that deserved discussion rather than turning someone's work into a public punching bag. I also felt regret because, while I didn't miss the opportunity to attack this particular cover, I also had neglected to say anything about the many constructive and helpful editions that preceded it—not to mention the other articles that appeared in the issue itself. This editor had only seen criticism from me and from many others who left comments on my social media posts. That isn't to say that I couldn't critique that cover without reading previous issues, but my perspective was limited. At the very least my discussion could have started in a more constructive place, acknowledging that, based on their previous work, I shared some common ground and beliefs with the editors, even if I took a different view about the message on the cover. That certainly would have offered a more constructive starting place than a barrage of comments writing off the magazine as garbage and the editors as out of touch.

Perhaps the most important question we can ask ourselves in our online interactions, especially among fellow Christians, is what our goals are. Are we seeking to make ourselves feel better or escape personal scrutiny by calling attention to the failures of someone else? Do we hope to change someone's mind or to at least add a perspective that this person may not have heard before?

As I apologized to this editor and nursed my regrets about my approach to social media, I realized that I had primarily succeeded in adding to the noise, anger, and division among Christians. If I wanted to change the discussion, I could have adopted a far more constructive approach that invited discussion while still asking hard questions. In addition, social media may still not have been the best venue for that kind of discussion, but I shouldn't have been surprised that my hot take resulted in an out-of-control fire among my social media network.

While I'm most familiar with the Protestant and evangelical debates on social media, I have also watched my Catholic friends attempt to navigate their toxic debates on social media between conservative and progressive Catholics. These divisions have been smoldering for generations, but social media has offered a perfect environment for them to flame into life. My Catholic grandfather railed against the reforms of Vatican II until his dying day, so it's no surprise to me that Catholics are divided on social media. Even Thomas Merton could write a sharp letter at times, calling one author's line of reasoning about emphasizing the active life over the contemplative life "utterly stupid."[11] Perhaps it's a good thing that Merton didn't have access to social media!

Ed Stetzer notes in his book *Christians in an Age of Outrage* that correcting one another online could consume more hours than a full-time job, and perhaps that kind of reality check can help us reconsider what we are hoping to accomplish in our online interactions. Perhaps it would help to ask how we can become more present in our communities, addressing injustice and inequality while sharing the good news of God's love, rather than policing what other Christians believe. If we do engage with each other online, are there ways we can share our own stories and perspectives that encourage dialogue and consideration? I have shifted my perspective on plenty of issues and beliefs over time, but it was always a gradual process in which I was exposed to new ideas, took time to consider them, and tried them on for size at my own pace. My own shifts and changes were never in response to hot takes, clapbacks, or being shamed on social media. While social media and digital technology in general are a great way to access lots of information and perspectives, they can unfortunately lead to exile from one another.

TECHNOLOGY EXILES US

The effect of technology often feels a bit like an exile from God, ourselves, and our neighbors. We can effectively share information on our devices and easily find the opinions of people we care about, but technology can also send us into a wilderness of the unreal where we aren't sure whether we're interacting with real people or at least the authentic versions of the people who created the profiles. We may not even be sure whether we're sharing our true selves with others or some fabricated image. Then again, even if we are sharing authentically, we can't say for sure whether an online connection is a truly deep connection with others unless we have a way to follow up with a more personal interaction—even an email, a text message, a phone call, or visit.

And still, others may not even see us as we are. They may affix stickers to us that categorize us. Some have spoken of the danger of labeling someone, but I think that a "sticker" metaphor is closer to what happens to the caricatures we carelessly slap onto each other on our screens. Someone may think they've got a handle on what every progressive Christian or conservative Christian thinks and believes, and so they begin placing these stickers on others and cutting short conversations, let alone their empathy and compassion, on the basis of these incomplete avatars.

Living in a very conservative state has been a needed challenge to move beyond my simplified characterizations of others. For instance, I can imagine that a discussion of climate change would go poorly on social media with some of my neighbors, as some even have "Friends of Coal" license plates at a time when our earth is warming rapidly and perhaps out of control. A pastor in our town quietly confided with me that he dare not post on social media about how badly his family needs the Affordable Care Act, which offers provisions for his preexisting medical condition. He doesn't know how they could otherwise afford healthcare, especially since his church didn't provide it for him.

What is it about our interactions on social media that keep us from seeing people with compassion and empathy as they live in fear of losing their healthcare or of a warming planet? Why are we struggling to have charitable debates on social media with people we care about?

The answer is that social media is functioning within its limits, but too many users expect us to somehow overcome this loss of empathy that comes from weaker online interactions that prevent us from being fully present. Conflict is almost inevitable in the online space because it disconnects us from flesh-and-blood people, from looking into their eyes, reading the expressions on their faces, hearing their tone of voice. We can focus on the content we post and how many likes or clicks we get while forgetting about the real people living with the consequences of our words, videos, or images. I have spent more than enough time regretting what I've posted online, especially when engaged in a debate or argument. My first instinct is rarely the right one in online interactions, and centering prayer has taught me to recognize when I'm entering into the wilderness of digital exile, seeing people in part but not truly interacting with them or helping them know that they are seen.

The good news is that we can make a habit of shifting our online interactions toward at least one personal interaction each day, such as a personal message or sharing how someone has helped us grow or learn. We can make more time for in-person interactions in order to hold on to our empathy and awareness of others that we've lost on our screens.

A study of fifty-one children, ages eleven and twelve, found that a week spent off their screens increased their ability to recognize the emotional cues of strangers. They spent a week at camp together, and at the start and end of the time, they took a diagnostic assessment of their ability to assess nonverbal behavior. Their error rate on the assessment decreased by 33 percent.[12] Hilarie Cash, clinical psychologist and founder of a rehabilitation program for video game addicts, emphasizes the importance of being in the same room with another person because of the consistent eye contact and the richness of the interaction. She compares our interactions via screens to eating candy. "It's a lot like feeding sugar to a hungry person," she said. "It's pleasurable in the short-term, but eventually they'll starve."[13]

Christians, thankfully, have the single greatest resource available at a time when so many people are starving for grounded, in-person interactions that offer more than the weak connections of social media and other digital tools. Many churches offer people a sacred space where we can be fully present for one another, make eye contact with each other, and show real love and concern for one another through prayer or in-person support, leading us out of the lonely exile of the digital wilderness. There are few other places available that can offer the same kind of reliable in-person support where people routinely show up week in, week out.

Unfortunately, the safe haven of the church is also becoming immersed in digital technology, both small screens and large screens. In many congregations, the race to adopt technology is on, and discipleship is becoming digitized in ways that could undermine the in-person, incarnational promises of ministry in a local church. How has the church adopted technology for better or for worse? What kinds of boundaries do we need around technology in our churches if we're going to preserve a space to reconnect with God and with each other?

. . . INVITATION TO RECONNECT . . . .

If you use social media this week, take note of how difficult or easy it is to pray. Are there any correlations between using social media and your ability to pray?

What are the "fruits" of social media and smartphones in your life?

This week, spend time with a friend or family member whom you don't normally see. How does this interaction shape how you view your week?

Solitude is the furnace of transformation.
Without solitude we remain victims of our society
and continue to be entangled in the illusions
of the false self.

—HENRI NOUWEN

FOUR

Where Two or Three Are Texting in My Name

Of the many examples of optimism for digital technology among Christian leaders today, the Church Tech Today website may be the most optimistic, offering a free guide to its subscribers: *How to Go from Zero to Hero with Instagram.* If only my kids knew that Instagram could turn them into heroes! I confess that I remain a bit skeptical of such lofty promises. While it's understandable that a church would use the latest social media technology to communicate and that communication experts could help them avoid major mistakes, there is a risk that churches are too optimistic about these tools and may even view them as neutral tools rather than as potentially disruptive to ministry or worship gatherings.

How could an Instagram Hero misuse social media in the context of the church? While the following story takes place before the dominance of Instagram, it very neatly fits the kind of usage an Instagram Hero may confront today.

Around 2011, I joined a group of writing friends in the back row of the STORY conference, a gathering for creative professionals in Chicago. In those days the event had a decidedly Christian feel to it, and a worship band opened several of the plenary sessions. As one of the more emotionally charged songs reached a crescendo, a guy in front of the stage lifted his arms in a giant V with his hands open to the heavens. I have no reason to doubt his sincerity in the moment, and I can't blame him for what happened next. A guy located a few rows ahead of us raised his smartphone, framing the man's outstretched arms over the sea of people as the band powered through the emotional bridge before roaring back to the chorus . . .

Click.

The image perfectly caught the power of the man's arms rising above the people, silhouetted against the serious worship band carrying on in the background, no doubt lost in the glory of the moment as the lights splashed radiance down on the stage.

I know this because a few hours later that image made the rounds on Twitter and Facebook. The caption read something like, "Incredible worship at the STORY conference!"

I'm still not sure what I think of that experience, but the least I can say is that it distracted me from the actual act of worship. I trust that the photographer didn't intend that result, even if he did hold his phone up in the view of hundreds of people. Without necessarily passing judgment, I at least want to ask whether taking pictures of our worship experiences for social media is helping us worship in the moment and to what extent we want to curate an image of our worship experience. It's true that photography can be a sort of contemplative art— even Thomas Merton took up photography, making peace with at least that small piece of technology. However, when it is time to enter a sacred space where our minds turn fully toward God, should we carry our little distraction machines with us?

This is something I thought about as I carried my phone with me as a substitute for my study Bible while attending a Vineyard church. When we moved to a new town and began attending an Episcopal church, where the bulletin mercifully provided the day's Scripture readings, I lost my reason to carry my phone with me into worship. The last thing I need during the liturgy is my smartphone. It adds nothing to the worship experience, and there are zero invitations to use it during the service. These days I stash it in our kids' art supply bag—which we always have on hand to keep them from crawling under the pews like ninjas on a secret mission.

To what degree should Christians in a digital culture, where people are spending significant time online, immersed in their computer, tablet, and smartphone screens, bring the Christian message onto these devices and even integrate these devices into their services? In what ways should great commission thinking send us into the social media space where so many people are having conversations, sharing information, and casually passing hours every week? Does the gospel message lose some of its effectiveness when it's shared via digital technology? Are we failing to critically examine the negative impact of technology on Christian community because we are too optimistic about and fascinated with its potential benefits?

With all the mental health, relationship, and empathy development issues taken into consideration, the implications for Christians are critical. Are we leaning too heavily on social media or online interactions in general to build shallow community online? Does our use of social media in a ministry context keep people at arm's length? Are we running the risk of minimizing the gospel into information that others literally download?

For the most part, the legacy of Billy Graham adapting the tools of technology, such as radio, television, and massive sound systems, has become the assumed norm, or at least a case study to learn from as many churches, especially American evangelical churches, bring more screens and technology into their buildings and apply online marketing strategies to outreach. Every piece of technology that we cart into our churches and plug into an outlet is viewed in the same way as Billy Graham switching from street corners to a stage with a microphone and then adding television cameras. While we may raise an eyebrow at smoke machines and complex stage lighting setups, there are other applications that also require more consideration, such as inviting social media engagement during a service, taking pictures to share from the service, sharing sermons on YouTube, playing videos during the service, or livestreaming video of a church service for another location. At the very least, most of the people attending church these days are carrying their portable distraction machines in their pockets, their purses, and perhaps even their faux leather Bible covers—I've been guilty. And who wouldn't carry a smartphone with a Bible app into church, with all the translations available to boot, rather than a hefty paper version? It just makes sense, right?

This use of social media has been further facilitated by easy access to Wi-Fi in many churches today. A 2017 LifeWay Research study found that 68 percent of Protestant congregations offer Wi-Fi for guests and staff and that 84 percent of churches have a website and Facebook page.[1] In addition, the Barna Group found in 2017 that 55 percent of Christians are reading the Bible digitally.[2] Churches are marching into the world of digital technology in order to read the Bible, to communicate with members, and to reach out to the community. Technology is already pervasive in our congregations, and the number of experts offering tips on using technology and social media more often and more "effectively" far outnumber the experts raising red flags. It's time to ask not only what we stand to gain by integrating technology into the church but what we stand to lose in our sacred spaces if we don't critically examine the impact of smartphones and social media on our congregations. If our Christian communities are going to help restore us from the fragmentation of technology and social media, we need to ask whether our worship gatherings are being undermined by technology in the first place.

I've been fortunate to attend a church that is relatively low-tech these days. Even if we did want to integrate more technology into our small congregation, we have enough low-tech members to keep us from jumping too far toward an immersion in technology. That is hardly the case for churches that cater to younger attendees or have been recently planted. I've worked in a small church that clawed and scraped for every bit of cost saving possible—we even bought generic coffee from the supermarket. Social media is too effective and too cheap to overlook when you're sweating the costs and the copyright laws of the images and song lyrics you project each Sunday. In addition, churches are challenged to keep up with the times. Expectations for many congregations in North America are shifting along with the culture, and that means more technology in our worship gatherings. Today, many evangelical and nondenominational worship services follow the trends of popular music, public speaking, leadership, and communication.

Technology decisions are woven into each of these dynamics, and the ever-present desire to remain relevant and to speak the language of the culture drives these assumptions.

The idea of silence or a low-tech worship experience isn't necessarily rejected. It's just rarely considered. The first time a leader set aside time during a worship service to sit in silence for ten minutes left me completely rattled. I had no idea what to do with myself. I didn't even know that sitting in silence could be "worshipful" or useful during a worship service. I had long missed out on the idea of sacred space or praying in silence.

Perhaps this idea of praying in silence is so challenging for churches to prioritize in part because they face significant pressure to become more connected and tech savvy, not less.

SOCIAL MEDIA–SAVVY MINISTRIES

No one would question a church listing its phone number and service times in a phone book. The telephone is a form of technology that we use to gather information, and so a church should make that easy to access. I don't think it's a stretch to view a church listing its service times, community programs, or other events on social media in the same light. For the most part, a church lists its events on these services because people can use them to find information. I'm more concerned about the next step that ministries take to increase engagement, to adopt marketing industry best practices for branding, and to create an experience, if not a spectacle, online. Besides our concerns about the invasion of technology into sacred space, we should also raise concerns about ministry becoming increasingly digitized without careful reflection on what is lost.

The two things I keep coming back to in my writing about technology, social media, and the church are the following:

The gospel isn't merely a message to be marketed.

At best, digital technology most often supplements Christian community.

The gospel is God's redemptive rule incarnated among us. When we proclaim that Jesus is Lord, that message is more than a slogan. It is the flesh-and-blood reality of God with us. As God is with us, we are linked together with Christ as our vine. Digital technology can help us communicate or learn about the needs of others, but will people truly feel that they are a part of a church if no one shows up to welcome them, break bread with them, or mourn with them in a time of need? Are pastors assuming that they've "ministered" to an individual, congregation, or the wider Christian community online when they've actually only made a weak connection via social media or reached more readers through a popular blog post?

For instance, a social media tool like Twitter was originally designed to simply share information—as in, where a group of friends were gathering to meet up. It was a bit like a group text. Posting the basic information about a church service time or a new ministry offering lands right in the wheelhouse of Twitter's original purpose. But how much more should churches rely on Twitter when it comes to ministering to others or building community?

At times, social media has replaced the traditional website for a business or a church. In the small town where I live, al-most every business in town relies on its Facebook page, to the point that some businesses won't answer their phones—but they'll reply instantly on Facebook Messenger. To what extent should churches immerse themselves in the social media game of creating viral content, curating exceptional photo shoots, or presenting a particular image of their ministry? Bob Carey, chair of the department of communication and new media at Gardner-Webb University in Boiling Springs, North Carolina, spoke about the quandary of using social media. "Simply opening an Instagram or Snapchat account isn't enough," he said. "Ministers must study the platforms and how they work. . . . If Instagram is the chosen platform for connecting with youth, churches and ministries should understand how hashtags work and seek to post relevant photos and videos." Carey even resorted to great commission language in his description of social media investment by churches. "I encourage you to count the cost," Carey said. "It's going to take time and effort to do this."[3]

I don't disagree with Carey that we need to consider ways to meet people where they are and to post in ways that effectively pass along information, but it's quite likely that some could take his advice in a way that leads toward a very steep cost. Churches' typical approach to outreach, church design, leadership, and communication has been to treat each practice as a neutral tool that can be applied without consequence to get the timeless gospel message out to the masses. The church simply adopts the best industry practices of each tool and then drops the gospel message into each application. If social media were a neutral tool, you would just need to learn how to use the tool and its tricks the way a woodworker learns how to use a chisel. However, the immersive, compulsive, and addictive qualities of social media and technology in general can run counter to the mission of the church to share the gospel message and to create a space for people to love God and to be physically present for people in need. Churches are being encouraged to get in on the game of distraction and curation, whether that means adopting strategies from leading brands, marketing firms, or social media influencers. At what point does this practice of creating engaging content, adding to the distractions and noise, or managing a particular "brand" image go too far for the people of God?

Perhaps I'm splitting hairs here, but I think there is a significant difference between a church that creates a simple video for their website that shows what a typical service is like and a church that uses a media team to create high-value video productions each week in order to drive more online engagement on Facebook, Instagram, and YouTube. Is online engagement the beginning and the end of the message and the church's relationship with viewers? While a video of a service can be useful for connecting with members when they're out of town or reaching those who are housebound, are the church's digital content strategies working within those targets? I would argue that some are playing the marketing influencer game at a high level, or at least wish they had the resources to up their game. In addition, there is a big difference between a church using Instagram to share pictures from an event and a church that carefully presents a perfectly curated image of relevance and style. The question is one of delivering style versus substance, of playing the social media game for keeps versus making in-person connections the primary aim and supplementing that with technology. The more invested a church becomes in online content marketing strategies, the greater the risk of losing sight of in-person interactions in favor of a branded, polished image designed for maximum engagement. While ministry certainly needs to make some changes with the times, Christians tend to overestimate what technology can do and to underestimate its potential harm in undermining ministry.

I've been reading many church technology blogs since 2010 and working in church communications since 2003. I endured the horror of editing church websites in Dreamweaver and have been involved in decisions about communication methods for congregations. While churches are often stereotyped as being behind the times when it comes to technology trends, my experience is that we're most worryingly behind in a critical analysis of technology and media. We have plenty of church-oriented blogs praising the ability to become a social media superhero and close to zero content warning about the potential pitfalls of social media or issues that may arise from adopting a content marketing plan for outreach or community building. I almost dropped my coffee with surprise when I read a post on the popular *unSeminary* blog that challenged churches to not use Facebook ads for their Easter services, since it is far more important to personally invite a friend to church than to rely on an ad—an opinion that was spot-on in my view.[4]

Our uncritical adoption of "best practices" from outside the church to advance our mission can undermine that very mission itself. Even the layout of most churches betrays just how much we rely on technology to accomplish our work for us, orienting everyone around a stage with screens, projectors, microphones, lights, and sound systems. Christians minister in the tension of a technology-driven context while sharing a very relational and personal gospel message where the Spirit is bestowed through the laying on of hands, not the swiping of a screen. To what degree do we give in to the norms and "best practices" of our times to connect with people instead of creating an alternative culture with minimal technology? Do digital technology's best practices undermine the church's best spiritual practices?

A pastor I know once put this tension between our dominant culture and an alternative church culture in rather striking terms for me. He had arranged the church "office" to look more like a living room and dining room than a typical business office space. In place of desks and cubicles, there were comfortable chairs in the front half of the room arranged in a semicircle and a large table in the other half of the room. There were a few filing cabinets off to the side and a room in the back with two sections for study, meetings, or private phone calls, but the emphasis of the primary space was relational, granting it an almost family-like atmosphere. When I mentioned my observation to him, he let out a deep sigh and said, "Thank you for noticing that. It's so important to me."

Many mornings I walk by a large church office where staff members are sitting at desks with their eyes glued to their computer monitors. I fully understand that there are emails to reply to, contacts to make, research to sort out, and writing to work on. However, has ministry been digitized to an extreme today, especially as many churches adopt a business approach to their ministry? Have we worked so hard to produce an experience on our screens in the sanctuary that we have overlooked the ways this means of communication and these types of worship experiences pull us away from in-person relationships?

The bigger a pastor or a ministry becomes on social media, the greater the pressure to maintain that image and to produce quality content. All manner of toxic problems can result if the maintenance of the brand image begins to overshadow other priorities, such as guarding the spiritual health of the pastor or serving the needs of the most vulnerable members of the congregation or community. At a certain point, churches who invest in social media will need to ask whether they are about spiritual formation in a beloved community or the digital conversion of an audience into fans.

RACE TO DISTRACTION

If we consider what we are lacking in most circumstances because of our smartphones, it's silence, freedom from distractions, and interpersonal conversations. The church can offer the very things that Sherry Turkle urges us to preserve in society: sacred space with a singular focus. A writer for *The Atlantic* summed up Turkle's prescriptions as: "Abandon the myth of multitasking for good—it is neither efficient nor conducive to empathy . . . and instead embrace 'unitasking,' one thing at a time." As Turkle notes with dismay, "We text during funerals. We text during religious services of all sorts. When I ask people why they do that, they admit it—they say, we text during the boring bits."[5] The question is warranted: Should we even have smartphones in our pockets or turned on when attending worship services? While we can use smartphones for greater convenience and efficiency, does having members alert and aware of their phones, say for a childcare update, pull them away from worship? We have managed to get by with large church meetings for generations without smartphones. Surely, we can make do without them in the future.

The deeper philosophical problem is how and if the church should embrace the culture as a means of reaching it and engaging it on its own terms versus providing an alternative subculture that can restore something that has been lost. We see this tension as churches try to attract youth with massive parties and social events. While there's nothing wrong with a party, social gathering, or potluck (provided you're not concerned about your cholesterol), the scale of these endeavors in our entertainment-saturated consumer culture could send a message that the church can give us what we want for amusement while slipping in some Christian messaging. We at least need to have conversations, in person preferably, about whether we need more screens with more weak connection options in our churches or whether we need to consider ways to offer our communities the resources of silence, focus, and interpersonal relationships that attendees may be lacking because of their immersion in digital devices. The church can become a haven to provide an alternative to digital distraction—using digital communication in a minimal and effective way when necessary. Rather than trying to compete with companies and corporations that have more resources, expertise, and staff, churches can depart the social media arms race and focus on what they do best: personally reaching out to people who need a loving God, offering a physical space for spiritual restoration, and reaching out to those who are suffering or struggling.

If we imagine digital formation and spiritual formation as competing forces in our lives, we may imagine them offering two different paths toward the goals of abundance and wholeness. Digital formation promises abundant life by making us more digitally connected with others and eliminating boundaries in our lives. The more information, the more friends, and the more notifications we have, and the more time we spend on our digital devices and social media apps, the more "abundant" our lives will be. While we can make important connections and learn vital information on social media, the true abundance comes in the form of data for mammoth corporations that convert that data into profit as advertisers sell more things to people who have been told what they lack and how the right product or app can meet their needs.

On the other hand, spiritual formation tells us that we already possess the abundance of God's presence through the promised Holy Spirit. What we often lack is clarity, focus, or time to become aware of what we already have. The more distracted we are, the harder it is to take part in the abundant life God has already given to us. From this point of view, we no longer have to view ourselves as competitors with the technological society. We don't have to master social media engagement to win people over; don't have to flood our sanctuaries with smartphones or turn to streaming video sermons by top-notch preachers. We also don't have to go low-tech in every circumstance, but at the very least, the pressure is off. Our mission isn't to win the distraction game. That's not our strength anyway.

The strength of the church is embodying a meaningful, life-changing alternative that no corporation can ever duplicate or trick us into creating.

The gift of the church for a world drowning in digital distraction is the spiritual restoration that comes from God's always present love.

If the church has one asset going for it, it's the fact that it offers a physical space where people reliably show up every week. That physical space does not need video screens, smartphones, or other forms of technology to accomplish its purpose, and if every scrap of technology were removed from most church sanctuaries, the experience on Sunday wouldn't necessarily suffer or change that much—at least it shouldn't.

We could immerse ourselves in more technology with video clips, animated song lyrics, apps on smartphones, and inspiring photos during the worship service, or by inviting social media posts during the sermon, but should we? People are already immersed in technology every day. Rather than trying to do technology like everyone else and risking the loss of attention, worship, or meditation, we can choose to go with minimal technology and focus on what we do best as a community.

Writing before the rise of digital technology, Howard Thurman noted that a time of quiet preparation was essential for prayer and held out hope that the church could provide that badly needed sacred space:

> Perhaps, as important as prayer itself, is the "readying" of the spirit for the experience. In such "readying" a quiet place is very important if not altogether mandatory. In the noise of our times such a place may be impossible to find. One of the great services that the Christian church can render to the community is to provide spells and spaces of quiet for the world-weary men and women whose needs are so desperate.[6]

Digital formation takes so much from us and may distract us from the life-giving practices of spiritual formation. If our religious communities don't help us value space for spiritual practices, who will?

As we step out of the immersion of digital formation, we have an opportunity to examine the goals and possibilities of spiritual formation. While we don't have to cut ourselves completely off from digital technology, we will most likely find that the goals of spiritual formation tend to run directly counter to those of technology. In addition, spiritual formation doesn't aim to take away the good things of digital technology. Rather, it aims to reconnect us with the good things God has already given us and intended for us—these are often obscured by digital technology. As we seek to make space to reconnect with these good things, let's consider why spiritual formation is worth preserving.

... **INVITATION TO RECONNECT** ....

Take note of how you interact with your smartphone in your religious community or church gathering this week.

When were you most drawn to use your phone during a worship service? In what ways did this make you more or less aware of others or of the worship service?

Commit to adding more distance between yourself and your phone at church or while attending a religious gathering, and pay attention to how that helps or hinders your worship experience.

At the center of our being is a point of nothingness which is untouched by sin and by illusion, a point of pure truth, a point or spark which belongs entirely to God, which is never at our disposal, from which God disposes of our lives, which is inaccessible to the fantasies of our own mind or the brutalities of our own will. This little point of nothingness and of absolute poverty is the pure glory of God in us. . . .

I have no program for this seeing. It is only given.

But the gate of heaven is everywhere.

—THOMAS MERTON

FIVE

The Goal of Spiritual Formation

Monks don't usually travel into the city in order to have a spiritual epiphany. Perhaps we imagine them venturing off into fields or forests, sitting in lofty stone chapels while chants echo off the walls, or kneeling at prayer in their austere cells. If anything, people in the city plan retreats to monasteries to get away from the pressure of daily life and to become more aware of God. It is no small irony that Thomas Merton's most significant spiritual epiphany occurred in the tree-deprived city of Louisville, rather than in his beloved woods around the Abbey of Gethsemani.

Merton had longed to become a hermit of sorts, often devising schemes to withdraw himself from the many noisy jobs that filled his day in the monastery. When selected for the task of marking trees in the woods for a forestry crew, he cheerfully set off in the woods with a hymn on his lips while the rest of the monks lumbered off to the farm fields where tractors roared all day. While the simple austerity of a cell in a community suited most monks, Merton craved his own hermitage off in the woods where he could pray and write without interruption. Later in his life he even investigated hermitage options in Alaska that he could use for part of the year. If anyone liked being alone to pray, it was Thomas Merton.

And yet Merton's most profound recorded religious experience happened in the heart of Louisville while surrounded by chattering people, sputtering cars, and looming buildings. While on a trip to run errands, Merton glimpsed the glory of God in the people all around him: "In Louisville, at the corner of Fourth and Walnut, in the center of the shopping district, I was suddenly overwhelmed with the realization that I loved all these people, that they were mine and I theirs, that we could not be alien to one another even though we were total strangers." Having devoted himself to contemplative prayer and silence before God, he discovered the profound mystery of humanity's God-given dignity: "I have the immense joy of being man, a member of a race in which God Himself became incarnate." While he glimpsed the beauty of God in the people all around him, Merton found himself profoundly aware of his obligation to devote himself to the benefit of others. The splendor of God in the people around him left a deep impression on him. As he wrote about his epiphany, "There is no way of telling people that they are all walking around shining like the sun."[1]

After this spiritual epiphany, Merton became more outspoken in his writing about war, pollution, greed, racism, and poverty. Many of his superiors resisted this shift in his writing, arguing that monks should only concern themselves with prayer. Walking a fine line between his perceived obligation to address the major issues of his time and his vow of monastic obedience, Merton never lost sight of his commitments to praying in solitude and advocating for justice and peace. The closer Merton drew to God, the more his spiritual formation led him to love and serve his neighbors.

SAVE US FROM ILLUSIONS AND DESTRUCTIVE ACTIONS

When Jesus spoke of his ministry, he compared himself to a doctor who came to heal those who were sick. What kind of sicknesses did he find? How did he deal with them? While I wouldn't rule out a prayer for healing when it comes to smartphone addiction, let's consider the types of heart issues, inner motivations, and actions that Jesus dealt with so that we can take a closer look at our own.

Looking at the gospels and epistles, I see two major heart problems that Jesus and his followers addressed: illusions and destructive actions. On the one hand, there were people who sinned or who felt distant from God because of an illusion or false narrative about themselves that Jesus challenged with an invitation to live by faith and to view God as a loving parent who could deliver them from the captivity of their thoughts. On the other hand, Jesus and his followers invited those engaged in destructive actions and systems, which harmed themselves or their neighbors, to stop indulging themselves and to love their neighbors as God loved them.

Starting with John the Baptist, he confronted the harmful actions and systems of the Roman soldiers and the illusions of the Jewish people who came to hear him preach. According to John, the Romans believed they were the conquerors who could exploit people, while the Jewish people were convinced they possessed the right spiritual pedigree, beliefs, and practices to assure themselves a place before God.

Jesus confronted the illusions of the woman at the well about God and herself while also inviting her to leave behind her destructive actions.

Jesus welcomed the change of heart in Zacchaeus, who voluntarily stopped his destructive actions in an unjust tax collection system. He also certainly left behind the illusions that wealth had given him.

Sadly, the rich young ruler clung tightly to his illusions about wealth, as he refused Jesus' invitation to follow him apart from his possessions.

Paul wrote to the Corinthians about their illusions of wisdom and their destructive practices that alienated the poor among them and led to factions in their community.

In each case, we see people who have been alienated from God, from one another, and from their true selves as God's beloved children being invited from the darkness of their illusions and harmful actions into the light of God. If spiritual formation is a process or journey of being conformed to the image of Christ as we begin to fully experience and enjoy the connection to God's love that already belongs to us, then it begins with an invitation. We have a starting point—you may call it a conversion—where we decide that the life of Christ in us, imparted through the Holy Spirit at Pentecost, is worthy of our attention and time. We can choose to begin clearing away space so that the life of Christ already imparted to us as a free gift can heal our wounds, correct our illusions, and reconnect us with the present love of God that can heal our divisions with each other. A common metaphor in Scripture for spiritual formation is a tree that is tended by an attentive gardener and produces fruit for the benefit of many. If we ignore or block the life of God in us and undermine the fruit that God's Spirit desires to bring about in our lives, then we will tragically miss our chance to know the security and peace of God's love that can permeate our relationships and actions.

The slow, steady, and patient approach of gardening offers a helpful picture of the process of spiritual growth. We begin by removing the weeds and anything else that may block the sunlight or threaten the roots of plants in the garden. Then, after planting, we enter a cycle of watering, weeding, fertilizing, and supporting the plants as they grow. The harvest is coming, but that time of abundance and celebration is preceded by the slow and steady faithfulness of simple daily practices that remove the barriers to growth and fruitfulness in God.

Howard Thurman insists that we don't lose ourselves in this surrender. Rather, God illuminates what we have always been in God. We lose our illusions, but those illusions weren't our true selves. The illusions are certainly part of our story, and we should remain gentle and gracious with ourselves rather than hiding in shame, but letting go of them can help us focus more perfectly on the light of God in our lives, revealing who we have always been. Thurman writes, "The dynamics inherent in the surrender become immediately available to the life of the surrendered person. His life is given back to him at another level. Literally he loses his life and finds it. In the surrender to God in the religious experience there is no loss of being but rather an irradiation of the self that makes it alive with 'Godness' and in various ways."[2]

Most importantly, this freedom in God is a gift that we have already been given. Taking our garden metaphor one step further, we could say that the seeds of God's life are already present within us and need only cultivation and exposure to God's light and living water in order to grow—although we have no guarantee what this "growth" will look like. We aren't "adding" something to our lives. We are allowing God's life already within us to flourish without hindrance. Thomas Merton speaks of this true identity as "hidden in God's call to my freedom and my response to him."[3] He adds, "'Finding our heart' and recovering this awareness of our inmost identity implies the recognition that our external, everyday self is to a great extent a mask and fabrication. It is not our true self. And indeed our true self is not easy to find. It is hidden in obscurity and 'nothingness,' at the center where we are in direct dependence on God."[4]

The goal of spiritual formation is to remove these barriers that obscure and restrain the present life of God in us. One of the most reliable ways that Christians have confronted the emptiness of the false self is removing themselves from the noise and distraction of daily life. Henri Nouwen writes in *The Way of the Heart* that "solitude is the place of the great struggle and the great encounter—the struggle against the compulsions of the false self, and the encounter with the loving God who offers himself as the substance of the new self."[5] As we let our narratives and inner chatter fade away, we are left with the discomfort of our emptiness, relying completely on God to supply something in its place. Nouwen adds, "The wisdom of the desert is that the confrontation with our own frightening nothingness forces us to surrender ourselves totally and unconditionally to the Lord Jesus Christ."[6]

The result of facing our illusions and distractions is a kind of purity of heart that doesn't come from imposing external rules, living in fear of an angry God, or forcing obligations on ourselves. The blossoming of the true self as revealed by God reconciles us to our illusions, even giving us compassion for ourselves. Spiritual practices such as prayer, silence, meditating on Scripture, or the mindfulness of the Examen (a daily review of where God may be present and how to pray) create space for God to replace our illusions and destructive practices with a purity of heart that flows from God's loving presence in us. Merton speaks of this inner purity flowing from the new self as an inner transformation: "It means the renunciation of all deluded images of ourselves, all exaggerated estimates of our own capacities, in order to obey God's will as it comes to us in the difficult demands of life in its exacting truth. Purity of heart is then correlative to a new spiritual identity—the 'self' as recognized in the context of realities willed by God."[7]

Being saved from our illusions about ourselves can help repair some of the ways our minds become filled with distractions that keep us from God and the gracious gifts God gives us. However, our illusions about ourselves are but one of the many sources of thoughts and narratives that can keep us from the spiritual restoration God offers us.

REMOVING BARRIERS FROM GOD

Since the age of eleven, I have never loved mowing the lawn. The only thing worse for my allergies would be sticking my head in a bag of cut grass. Still, I wasn't doing myself any favors when I began stewing over the latest social media or news outrage while mowing the lawn. I have no idea why I afflicted myself in this way. Although some mental space can be helpful for facing the toxic or draining thoughts in my mind, mowing became my "angry time" where I fixated on an injustice or harmful action I heard about in the news. My angry time became a symptom of a bigger problem: excessive time on social media had filled my mind with thoughts that I struggled to process, let alone trust to God.

Considering that digital formation either fills our minds with thoughts or prevents us from facing our thoughts in silence, spiritual formation frees us from the constant chatter of our thoughts and trains us to let go of them. Whether we are meditating on the life-giving words of Scripture or waiting in silence before God, spiritual formation relies on disengaging from the constant flow of chaotic ideas that press us toward a reactive mind. In addition, once we have stepped away from this stream of ideas, we also need to let go of the ones that we have fixated on.

The thoughts lodged in our minds prevent us from perceiving ourselves and God's presence clearly. The more we are engaged in stimulation and ideas, the less space we'll have to thoughtfully review our days and to let go of what Martin Laird calls "afflictive thoughts." These thoughts can fill our minds to the point that we fail to realize God is present, or we remain boxed in by our illusions about ourselves or God. By sitting in silence, releasing our thoughts gently, and creating space for God, we can gain greater clarity through simple contemplative practices. Laird writes, "Contemplative practice gradually dispels the illusion of separation from God. Through the medicine of grace, the eye of our heart is healed by the gradual removal of the lumber of mental clutter, 'the plank in our eye' that obscures the radiance of the heart. This radiance is a ray of God's own light."[8]

This letting go of thoughts is not a spectacular or brand-new, cutting-edge spiritual practice. This isn't the sort of thing spiritual gurus do onstage to the applause of the crowd. It is an ancient spiritual practice of letting go of our thoughts and illusions that can blind us to the brilliance of God—even if the practice often feels quite unspectacular on most days. Howard Thurman shares how the unspectacular waiting in silence, releasing each thought as it comes, is the kind of space that God can work with in our lives: "It is in the waiting, brooding, lingering, tarrying timeless moments that the essence of the religious experience becomes most fruitful. It is here that I learn to listen, to swing wide the very doors of my being, to clean out the corners and the crevices of my life—so that when His Presence invades, I am free to enjoy His coming to Himself in me."[9]

If smartphones and social media ensure that we never have to wait in boredom, that we can always find a source of stimulation, and that we never have to be alone with our thoughts, we are training ourselves to fail in spiritual formation. In fact, our devices are stealing an important element of a typical prayer experience. Put bluntly, prayer is often quite simple and mundane, and even boring. It may include incredible encounters with God or moments of powerful transformation, but the day-in, day-out discipline of prayer is rarely exciting or even rewarding. Prayer even thrives in the boredom of its simple routines and practices.

Laird assures us with the following praise for boredom:

> We do well to recall that boredom is often the work of grace within our practice and a sign of crucial deepening beyond what our senses can grasp. Since God cannot be grasped in the way perceptible objects can, boredom serves to wean us away from equating union with God and feelings of God's presence as a state of constant peace and recollection. These feelings are impermanent, patterns of weather but not the mountain itself.[10]

We can swing between two extremes in our approach to prayer. On the one hand, some Christians expect the spectacular moment of deliverance or conversion to carry them from one new level of spiritual vitality to another. To fail at gaining that dramatic connection with God can only spell failure in their spiritual practices. On the other hand, some Christians emphasize the "strangely" part of Methodist leader John Wesley saying his heart was "strangely warmed" during his conversion experience. Any kind of emotional experience or sense of the Holy Spirit at work is written off as a trick of the mind or heart. Some even assert that a spiritual experience is the sign of darker forces at work. Contemplative teachers remind us that what we think or feel doesn't change the reality of God's presence in our lives, so regardless of whether we have a spiritual encounter, we can gently release these thoughts and rest in the quiet hope of God.[11]

While we can create space in our minds and lives for God, and we can grow in our awareness of God, we can't necessarily get any closer to a God who is already present through the indwelling Holy Spirit. The Holy Spirit is given by grace, and there aren't ways to upgrade the dwelling of the Holy Spirit. There's only one Spirit. At times it can seem that some people have a better version of the Holy Spirit. Rather, we have different spiritual gifts and expressions of those gifts, but God's gift of the Spirit does not depend on our emotions or experiences. God is already present when we pray, but our awareness can become a battlefield of sorts.

Prayer is a surrender to God, a consenting to God's presence, and a great act of faith. Contemplative teachers often use the word *intention* to describe our posture of being aware of and available to God. There surely are times when we will become emotional, sense a message of direction from God, or even feel directed to pray in a specific way. These are excellent, life-giving expressions of prayer, but we can make the mistake of elevating these moments above the simple, everyday practice of waiting in silence before God. Both forms of prayer are a surrender, and we run the risk of missing the opportunities for growth and formation that come in silence if we expect something to "happen" each time we sit before God in a time of quiet.

Merton writes in *Contemplative Prayer* that our great danger in prayer is that we can begin to examine our minds in search of some kind of stimulation or result. This temptation becomes all the greater when we have grown so accustomed to stimulation and results from our activity. We often do things because we expect them to make us feel different, hopefully better, even if their promises of satisfaction are fleeting and unfulfilling. Author Cynthia Bourgeault assures us that simple prayer practices such as centering prayer are far from result-based. In fact, the benefit of a simple practice like centering prayer accumulates and grows over time. We are most likely to observe this in our interactions with others.

RELATE WITH COMPASSION AND MERCY

Besides removing ourselves from the many thoughts afflicting our minds, including those supplied by the social media ecosystem and constant access to breaking news, our spiritual formation practices can train us to move beyond our reactive, defensive responses to others. Silence before God can help quiet our fears and give us the space to let thoughts be without reaction. This can disarm the thoughts that would typically unsettle us and make us combative toward others. Martin Laird sees contemplation as a way to remove ourselves from our self-centered default settings that fear what could happen to us and to open our minds to the experiences and needs of others. "By learning to choose what we give our attention to," he writes, "we open ourselves up to the possibilities of experiencing a situation with less anxiety and with more compassion."[12] Rather than existing in a state of reaction, we can let thoughts be and free ourselves to see the needs, fears, and hopes of others. Besides preserving our own energy and creating space for presence before God, contemplation and silence become critical tools for growing our awareness of and compassion for others around us.

Letting go of our thoughts in contemplation isn't necessarily the same as having no thoughts. Rather, Laird assures us that the practice helps us let go of the thoughts that would pull us away from being fully present with God: "Returning and returning and returning without a speck of any expectation of results." Over time, the fruits of this practice will become apparent: "Practice gradually trains the attention and grounds us more solidly in our bodies, increasing our ability to be where our bodies are at any given moment."[13] Laird is making a statement that is as practical as we can hope for when our screens continually pull our attention away from the solid dirt, flesh-and-blood, blue skies, wind, and sunshine of our world. As our screens promise us rewards and connections that disconnect us from our feelings, fears, and the physical objects right in front of us, contemplation forces us to fully feel our bodies, to face our fears, and to examine who we are and how we relate to others.

As contemplative prayer helps us face the fears and anxieties afflicting our minds, we'll be empowered to ask where they come from and what they are based on. More importantly, contemplative practice helps us get to the root of that which drives so many of the divisive, destructive, and even potentially violent narratives in our social media–information environment. "Contemplation," Laird writes, "liberates us from the seeds of violence in our own heart, especially from our individual and social compulsions to find someone to blame for the ills that befall us—such compulsions do nothing but keep us bent over on ourselves, blind to what constitutes a human."[14]

The goal of contemplation is increased awareness of and union with God, so any other benefit should not become the primary goal. However, as we seek to liberate ourselves from the formative aspects of digital technology, especially social media, so that we can enjoy the liberation of spiritual formation, contemplation becomes an essential piece of the puzzle. While digital technology trains us to crave stimulation, distraction, and emotional highs, spiritual practices such as contemplation can train us to crave silence and presence instead. It is an essential part of settling our minds, grounding us in truth, and even preparing us for action.

When Merton first entered the monastery at Gethsemani, he noted that its prayers were holding the nation together.[15] Something he experienced radiated out and extended into society for its benefit and peace. Prayer can do more than hold us together. It can hold our society together as we grow in compassion and mercy for each other. That doesn't stop us from speaking the truth about deception, racism, xenophobia, or other forms of bigotry. Rather, by stepping away from the perpetual cycle of rage and anger in the news and on social media to pray in silence before God, we can begin to see our neighbors through the compassionate eyes of God and join them in taking action to change unjust systems or meeting the needs of our communities.

Starting with the peace of our minds that can then flow out through our actions, prayer can also connect us with the desires of God for ourselves and for our neighbors. When we connect with the heart of God for others, we will find a means of loving others, for they are beloved children of God just as we are. The lines of separation, fear, and anger are challenged by the present love of God for us and for others. That isn't to say that developing inner peace and a capacity for love and empathy will solve all our problems. It's more likely that contemplative teachers like Merton or Laird would argue that they provide the inner stability for peace—we become peaceful, loving people who are then empowered from within to act for the benefit of our neighbors, who also bear God's beloved image. Nouwen writes, "Solitude molds self-righteous people into gentle, caring, forgiving persons who are so deeply convinced of their own great sinfulness and so fully aware of God's even greater mercy that their life itself becomes ministry. . . . When we are filled with God's merciful presence, we can do nothing other than minister because our whole being witnesses to the light that has come into the darkness."[16]

Notably, the judgment of Matthew 25 was based on the capacity of people to see Jesus in the people they served. Jesus will say, "For I was hungry and you gave me food, I was thirsty and you gave me something to drink, I was a stranger and you welcomed me, I was naked and you gave me clothing, I was sick and you took care of me, I was in prison and you visited me" (Matthew 25:35-36). Preserving each person's God-given human dignity is far from a radical idea in light of the biblical witness. If anything, Jesus wants us to take things a step further. He has incarnated himself with humanity, identifying with the people around us, especially those suffering the most.

As we pray and seek God in silent solitude, we can become aware of the loving presence of God in our world and will be more likely to recognize this presence even in the people around us.

Progressing forward with the aims of spiritual formation, we can see that being delivered from our illusions, leaving our afflictive thoughts behind, and growing in compassion will put us in a very different position than that established by the limits of digital formation through digital technology. A gentleness and peace will begin to flow from our lives when we move from reaction to reception of God's presence. If we can unplug ourselves from our devices and apps long enough, we can be shaped by God's loving presence. Laird writes, "Receptive mind receives in such a way that it gives. It does this without trying to, simply because it is its very nature to give."[17] Rather than adopting a reactive, fearful, and combative posture toward others, we will free ourselves to see others with greater empathy. As we become aware of the needs of others, grow in God's love, and preserve time to become present for them, we will be in a much better position to serve others.

PRAYER CAN PREPARE US FOR ACTION

If we are creating space for God and growing in our awareness of God, the resulting change in our lives and the fruit of the Spirit will lead us toward others. Spiritual formation shapes the actions we take and the people we serve because the God who shapes us cares deeply for our neighbors. The fruit of the Spirit is given to us so that it can be shared freely. I have personally felt the temptation to only view my contemplative practices as relevant for my relationship with God and mental health. *As long as I feel good about God, there is no need to act further.* In fact, serving others is costly and difficult, requiring awareness of suffering and sacrifices that I'd rather not make sometimes. And even if I do engage in meeting the needs of others as a response to my contemplative practices, it's not uncommon for some people to tell me, "Stick to prayer!"

Self-awareness can turn into self-centeredness, and in a consumer society where anything can become commodified, that is a real challenge in the contemplative practices of any faith. Writer David Rakoff noticed this when he attended a Buddhist retreat center for a weekend. While the weekend was devoted to developing compassion, he noted there had been no mention of current events or applying the weekend's teaching to how he interacted with others. As Rakoff discussed a disturbing event in Albania during a meal at the retreat center, one person at his table replied, "I'll say that this gives me *agita*. When things get heavy, I can't eat. Can we talk about something else?"[18] I have found similar temptations when practicing Christian contemplation. While there is a time for silence and focus on the presence of God, that isn't an invitation to limit our focus to merely our own horizons.

Writing about prayer for his fellow monks, Thomas Merton offered a vision of Christian prayer that was far from self-indulgent. Rather, it calls for a surrender and conversion experience where there is a "deep change of heart in which we die on a certain level of our being in order to find ourselves alive and free."[19] From this surrender and movement toward freedom comes a God-inspired shift in focus from our own needs to the needs of others. Merton adds, "I must use my freedom in order *to love*, . . . directing my love to the personal reality of my brother [and sister], and embracing God's will in its taken, often impenetrable mystery."[20]

The silent communion with God that we find by faith as we practice contemplative prayer isn't a nifty add-on for Christians seeking to bump their commitment to the next level. It's not a specialty for the monastic religious professionals. It's a simple, deeply rooted practice that belongs to the heritage of every Christian and can enable the other practices and mission of our faith. The then archbishop of Canterbury Rowan Williams shared:

> Contemplation is very far from being just one kind of thing Christians do: it is the key to prayer, liturgy, art and ethics, the key to the essence of a renewed humanity that is capable of seeing the world and other subjects in the world with freedom—freedom from self-oriented acquisitive habits. . . . To put it boldly, contemplation is the only ultimate answer to the unreal and insane world that our financial systems and our advertising culture and our chaotic and unexamined emotions encourage us to inhabit. To learn contemplative practice is to learn what we need so as to live truthfully and honestly and lovingly.[21]

If our spiritual formation practices are being undermined by uncritical use of digital technology, then we will lose out on the practices of prayer, meditation, and silence. These are the daily spiritual disciplines that have helped Christians remain united with a present God and have empowered them to live the Christian life. Losing our daily grounding in God's presence and the spiritual transformation that the Spirit brings deprives us of the life of Christ that can make us compassionate, loving, and full of the fruit of the Spirit for the benefit of others. If our minds are trained to expect stimulation, immediate feedback, and unfocused wandering, we can undermine the stability found in spiritual practices. Since we are surrounded by technology and the temptation of social media, creating space for spiritual practices will require some intention and planning. Now that we have a handle on the value of spiritual formation and its goals, we'll consider some simple ways to reconnect with spiritual formation and to resist the distractions of technology. The ideas in the chapter that follows will help you begin to create space for spiritual formation practices. Then we'll discuss some practical ways to make spiritual formation a regular habit and practice in your life while still using technology in a limited (hopefully very limited) capacity.

... INVITATION TO RECONNECT ....

Which illusion or misconception about yourself is social media most likely to reinforce?

When are your thoughts most often disrupted, uneasy, or angry? What do you think is the most likely cause of those thoughts?

How can you respond when you sense that your thoughts are becoming reactive?

The closer one approaches to God,
the simpler one becomes.

—SAINT THÉRÈSE OF LISIEUX

SIX

Detoxing from Distractions

A digital detox means different things for different people and could last for as little as a day or as long as a full month—some have even gone for a year. For me, it means avoiding social media, news websites, and excessive email checking that became habits for any quiet moment in my life. For one mom I know, it means putting boundaries around the deluge of text messages she receives from friends each day that fragments her attention for her kids. For some teenagers I know, a detox means stepping away from the pressure to get a certain number of likes for an image. Several single adults have mentioned taking steps to counteract the constant draw of checking a dating app. In each case, a technology detox reminds us what life can be like apart from the influence of a digital device or social media.

Not all detoxes offer the same insights. One technology writer, for example, found that giving up his phone for a day resulted in the *incredible, deeply engaging* sensory experience of holding coins . . . in his hand . . . and *rattling* them into the tip jar after paying for his coffee with cash. If that blows his mind, my kids would happily tell him about the epic splashes from tossing change into the fountain at the mall. Rather, we're after a deeper examination of our souls with and without technology. For instance, during the early years of our two oldest children, Facebook became a place I turned to for distraction when they drained me. That habit didn't really restore me, and over time, checking Facebook became more of a regular habit and distraction than an occasional break. Removing Facebook from my phone and tablet while also blocking the news feed and limiting my time on my laptop helped detox me from the daily distraction of Facebook so I could pay better attention to my kids and seek better restorative habits on challenging days.

START WITH A DIGITAL DETOX

A friend of mine was emotionally exhausted after doing online dating for two years. She checked notifications for as many as five sites a day, and she had one particularly rough week of relational bumps and bruises. Marjorie had taken "Sabbath" breaks from the apps on Sundays, and even limited use until the evening hours on weekdays, but she knew in her spirit that more was needed. With a mixture of hesitation and relief, Marjorie decided to disable her dating apps for a month. While she missed them at first, not having to deal with the constant demand of winks and likes and messages quickly became a welcome refuge. When Marjorie did return to the apps, she not only felt refreshed from the digital detox, but also felt a clearer sense of God's presence in her life—with or without apps.

Making any kind of meaningful and long-lasting change to address digital formation versus spiritual formation calls for a clear and decisive choice. If digital technology is designed to be compulsive, addictive, and invasive and we struggle to put our devices down because of their appealing connections, then we won't stand a chance without an intentional plan moving forward. Regaining the freedom to choose how we use social media and digital technology while cultivating space in our lives for spiritual formation won't be easy without some simple, concrete steps in place.

In fact, our situation is particularly urgent because many of us simply don't know how deeply we've been changed by digital formation. For instance, do we even know what a moment of silence can feel like when we're at peace and rest, or are we at the mercy of anxious thoughts to the point that we feel dependent on our phones or social media to save us from the discomfort of our own minds? I remember the agony of spending five minutes in silence when I first started practicing the Examen and contemplative prayer each evening. Getting to the point of sitting in silence for twenty minutes felt like an enormous test of my willpower at first. Before I tried periods of silence, though, I didn't really think it would be that hard. However, once I faced my dislike of silence and stillness, I could finally begin to ask how digital technology and social media had contributed to my restlessness and apparent need for stimulation. Until I stepped away from digital devices and apps, I couldn't fully understand how appealing and influential they had become in my life.

The vast majority of digital device and social media users need to consider their values for digital device usage, to go through some kind of detox, or to dramatically increase their barriers to social media use. There is no other way forward.

From the advice of business gurus to spiritual masters, a detox period is one of the most effective ways to truly gain control over the pull of our digital devices. That may be disturbing or disconcerting for you to read. I promise that while this may appear quite hard at first, it is a proven path that is supported by research, spirituality practitioners, and productivity experts. Whether that means limiting access by deleting social media from your portable devices, taking evenings or weekends (or both) off from social media, leaving your phone behind for errands around town, ending phone use at a set time each evening, or following a more complete fast for a period of time (whether one day or thirty days), a detox will help you recognize how your life is better or worse with constant access to social media and digital devices.

Spiritual formation author and speaker Richard Foster writes about facing the challenge of digital distraction with ascetic practices: "We need a discerning, life-giving technological asceticism. . . . If we will fast from food periodically it will help to temper the spirit of constantly grasping for control, and this will make it easier for us to fast from technology now and again."[1] Productivity expert Cal Newport suggests in *Digital Minimalism* that the most effective way to evaluate the impact and usefulness of social media and any other digital tool or app is to fast from it for thirty days without announcing your absence. Newport argues that if thirty days pass and you haven't missed out on anything vitally important and you find yourself having more time for in-person relationships, personal hobbies, or sustained attention at work, then it may be worth removing some of those digital tools. If thirty days seems too big a leap at first, consider going off social media for the weekend to see what a few days feels like. You could also remove social media apps from your phone for those thirty days and then use a blocking extension in your browser, like SelfControl or StayFocusd, to set up long-term blocks throughout the day or limit your usage on social media to set amounts of time. The key, according to Newport, is to avoid periods of limitation followed by periods of bingeing. This is why a thirty-day fast is often most effective.

The goal for most of us isn't to completely give up social media or smartphones. The goal is to gain an honest assessment of how these tools enhance or harm our most important relationships, tasks, and spiritual practices. We won't be motivated to make healthy changes unless we have realistic "before" and "after" images in our minds. Once we know how we feel under the influence of digital technology and how we feel apart from it, we'll be able to make informed, intentional choices about how much we consume (or how much we are consumed by these devices!), and then measure its impact so that we can freely choose how much is good for us. A social media or digital technology "diet" is used by some to explain a more sustainable long-term approach, even if a time of detox may help us with a reset.

Researchers for a 2018 study concluded that limiting the use of social media to no more than thirty minutes a day "may lead to significant improvement in well-being." Working with 143 undergraduates, researchers found that students who limited their use of Facebook, Instagram, and Snapchat to thirty minutes a day for three weeks had significant reductions in loneliness and depression compared with a control group that made no changes to their social media diet. Researchers noticed something else that happened when students self-monitored their time on social media. Just being mindful of screen time turned out to be beneficial. Students showed "significant decreases in anxiety and fear of missing out," a side effect of increased self-monitoring, noted researchers. As one study participant put it, "I ended up using [social media] less and felt happier. . . . I could focus on school and not [be as] interested in what everyone is up to."[2] An app like Moment can track your daily screen time, app usage, and number of phone pickups, offering updates throughout the day to help you regulate your usage.

Detoxing from social media for set periods of time and setting boundaries can help us determine what we will choose to include in our lives based on how it helps or harms us. Then we can enjoy social media and smartphones within set limits rather than relying on impulses and emotional swings, where social media or digital devices become just one of the ways we numb ourselves or escape our dislike of silence or boredom. Once we have a handle on our lives apart from the influence of digital formation, we can get to the root issues that social media and smartphones tend to exploit in our lives.

GETTING TO THE ROOT OF OUR STRUGGLES

I have delayed a closer examination of our reasons for misusing or overusing social media and our devices because I first wanted to get a handle on the design and aim of technology today. Christians especially can make the mistake of starting and stopping their examination of digital technology by looking at our personal responsibility apart from the aims of the makers of devices and apps. Now that we have a better idea of the ecosystem created by technology and media, we can face our own reasons for immersing ourselves in it and work toward greater freedom in determining what we will and won't use, as well as which blocks and boundaries will be most helpful.

Most importantly, I want to help us get to the root of our social media use or misuse. For instance, some people may turn to social media as a way to connect with people because they feel isolated and want to build a community. There could be positive and healthy ways to do this, particularly for individuals with disabilities or in situations that make it difficult to leave the house. In addition, someone working through a private struggle or confidential family matter may find wisdom and support in a private group or the shared experiences that others post online. On the other hand, some people who feel lonely could turn to social media regularly enough that it could prevent them from making deeper, meaningful connections with people in their communities as they settle for the weaker, less present, and less costly ties that come through their screens. Seeking connection in the face of loneliness is a good thing, but social media isn't always the best place to turn. Rather, it is often the easiest place to turn, but it doesn't necessarily address the root need of being seen, receiving interpersonal eye contact, experiencing empathy, being hugged, or receiving some other form of personal affirmation.

The times when I am most likely to overuse or misuse social media or my smartphone are typically when I am stressed out, too busy, bored, or anxious. Social media on my phone provided a portable escape pod for the times when I was struggling to remain present in the moment. In the past, social media offered a pleasurable distraction for a few minutes when I worked at a high-conflict workplace. Picking up my smartphone became a habit of sorts whenever I encountered something disturbing or worrying. Left unchecked, my social media and smartphone use became a habit that extended even into the times when I felt calm and balanced. It was the first, easiest thing to do regardless of my circumstances because it had become associated with calm or escape—even though it primarily offered distraction and did nothing to resolve the stress of my circumstances.

Getting to the *why* of my social media and digital device use has helped me realize that we shouldn't merely address our usage tendencies with blocks—as effective as they can be. We need to address the root issues that drive our use and our over-use. These are the very things we need to reflect on, seek sup-port for in our communities, and offer to God in prayer. It's not enough to say that a person who is alcoholic should stop drinking or that a person addicted to drugs should put aside marijuana. Each of these often serve as coping mechanisms for unaddressed pain. In particularly challenging situations, the reasons for substance abuse could range from watching their child suffer from a serious illness, losing a loved one suddenly, or coping with a form of abuse or relational turmoil. It's likely that in most cases our misuse or behavioral addictions to smart-phones aren't rooted in matters quite so serious. Nevertheless, if we want to give ourselves the best possible chance to remain in control of our devices and apps so we can live in the freedom that God promises, we will need to get down to the root of our behaviors. We can recognize that we may be more distracted or plugged in than we would prefer, but it takes ongoing soul work and examination to uncover the driving forces in our lives behind our usage habits.

While stress, personal trauma, or anxiety may not drive all of us in our smartphone or social media misuse, wider cultur-al trends may be at work within us. For instance, we may be driven to pursue constant connection because it feels produc-tive and useful for our work. With our digital devices we can al-ways engage in something that feels useful and productive, even when we are sitting alone in a restaurant. Howard Thurman urges us to consider a different perspective in our pursuit of rest and solitude that is much more along the lines of the monk standing in the field in the *In Pursuit of Silence* documentary. Thurman writes:

> We must lose our fear of rest. There are some of us who keep up our morale . . . by being always busy. We have made a fetish of fevered action. We build up our own sense of security by trying to provide a relentless, advantageous contrast between ourselves and others by the fevered, intense activities in which we are engaged. Actually, such people are afraid of quiet. Again, most activities become a substitute for the hard-won core of purpose and direction.[3]

Stopping and sitting in silence doesn't just feel bad because it feels unproductive. Sitting in silence with our own thoughts can also feel terrifying because we typically face our fears in silence. At the risk of putting too fine a point on this, finally stopping for a moment of quiet can serve as a reminder of the ultimate moment when we stop and let go of our grip on this life. It's bad enough that sitting in silence to pray feels unproductive. It's worse because we might have to face our looming existential dread. Thomas Merton notes, "I cannot discover my 'meaning' if I try to evade the dread which comes from first experiencing my meaninglessness! . . . One reason why our meditation never gets started is perhaps that we never make this real, serious return to the center of our own nothingness before God. Hence we never enter into the deepest reality of our relationship with him."[4]

The path forward here isn't easy. As we face silence and solitude apart from the buzzing of our phones and the appealing options on our screens, we may not like what we find at first. Our busy lives or engagement in technology can become a mask to cover up the things we're running from each day. Some of our dread, fear, and anxiety may call for professional help, while other sources of anxiety and fear may be addressed if we can open our sources of pain to God in prayer and share about them with others. In facing my own sources of pain and anxiety, I have benefited from a combination of silent prayer, journaling, intercessory prayer from my Christian community, spiritual direction, and professional help.

Whatever your reasons for overusing or misusing your smartphone or social media for distraction, the goal here is to establish a personal baseline for health and spiritual well-being. When I feel drawn to overuse my phone or social media, I know that either I'm most likely in a stressful situation or my schedule has filled up and crowded out my spiritual practices. Mind you, I have a pile of blocking apps and policies that help me avoid overusing social media (more about that in the resources section in the back of this book), but when addressing root causes, the times when I'm most drawn to social media or smartphone use are the times when I need to examine myself. I may be avoiding a challenging project, worn out by a parenting situation, or stressed about something I read on a news website. Then again, I may be anxious about something I read on social media. Regardless, turning to social media or disconnecting from reality by reading a bunch of articles or personal updates on social media will hardly address the deeper issues in my life that are driving my activity. Without stepping back for a time of assessment, I'll continue to be at the mercy of my root causes and left wondering why it's so hard to exert self-control in my life.

We can only avoid the pain and anxiety of our lives for so long before it shows up. However, once we know what we're up against, the Christian practice of contemplative prayer helps us face the disruptions of our thoughts and then let go of them so we can entrust ourselves to God. This is hardly a delusion or avoidance. Rather, we can begin to see our thoughts for what they really are and can then create space for God to work in our lives. Through contemplative prayer, we can begin to find our stability again in the present love of God for us. This is where spiritual formation can help us begin to grow into the health and abundance that Jesus promised.

RELEASE DISTRACTING THOUGHTS

Contemplative prayer is the simple and ancient Christian prayer practice of making space for God in our lives so that we can increase our awareness of the spiritual work God is already doing in us. Contemplative prayer itself is God's work, but we can use silence, breathing, a prayer word like *beloved*, or a prayer phrase like "Lord Jesus" or "Lord have mercy" to still our minds before God. Merton writes, "*Prayer* then means yearning for the simple presence of God."[5] I like to think of this as preparing a space in my life for God.

Contemplative prayer is a surrender and gentle consent to God, allowing God to move as God sees fit. Howard Thurman gets to the heart of this act of surrender in this preparation work when he writes, "I work at preparing my mind, my spirit for the moment when God comes to Himself in me. When it happens, I experience His Presence. When this experience becomes an object of thought and reflection, it is then that my mind creates dogmas, creeds and doctrines. These are the creations of the mind and are therefore always after the fact of the religious experience."[6]

Centering prayer is one contemplative prayer practice that frees our minds from distractions and entanglements so that we can increase our awareness of God's presence by using a simple prayer word or phrase to center on God alone. The word or phrase offers our busy, always engaged minds something to do while we create space for God's Spirit. Saint Diadochos of Photiki shared about using a prayer word while working or praying in solitude: "The intellect requires . . . some task which will satisfy its need for activity. For the complete fulfillment of its purpose we should give it nothing but the prayer 'Lord Jesus.'"[7] Since the Holy Spirit already dwells within us and prays on our behalf, contemplative prayer practices won't add more of God's presence. Rather, contemplative prayer practices can add more of our own awareness to what God is doing in our lives. We can more fully enjoy and participate in the life of God that is already in us. Martin Laird writes that "we cooperate with what grace is already trying to clear."[8] Contemplation addresses the thoughts that prevent us from fully joining in what God is doing. The more entangled we become with social media debates, reactions to the news, and ongoing conversations that take up our time each day, the harder it will be to disengage from the chatter of the day in order to enjoy God's peaceful and restorative presence.

A significant amount of ink has been spilled (and digital device storage taken up) by books that seek to help us disengage from the chatter of our thoughts and pressure of our fears that make it so difficult to pray. Many of the most widely read authors today, including Thomas Keating, Cynthia Bourgeault, and Martin Laird, have adapted the teachings of the anonymous Carthusian monk who wrote *The Cloud of Unknowing* in the fourteenth century. Clearing away the clutter of distracting or afflictive thoughts is nothing new! Christians since the earliest desert fathers and mothers have struggled to step away from disorienting thoughts in order to become more fully present for God in prayer. This practice of releasing thoughts has been so enduring and common for Christians through the centuries because it is a challenging discipline that remains deceptively simple in its substance. Much like taking up a daily discipline such as running, it is simple to do but hard to find the daily willpower. If we persevere in it, we will grow in our strength and ability to let go of our thoughts and remain more fully present and aware of God. Laird writes the following about the challenges of releasing distracting thoughts:

> The practice of contemplation is not an attempt to have no thoughts. This only serves to build up tension in the body and keep us forever checking to see if we're having any thoughts. This in turn increases the momentum of reactive mind and the lifestyles born of it (their numbers are legion). The practice is returning and returning and returning, without a speck of any expectation of results (mercifully, results are often kept out of our sight; otherwise we would be forever journaling about them). Practice gradually trains the attention and grounds us more solidly in our bodies, increasing our ability to be where our bodies are at any given moment.[9]

If we can see the way that social media can, in a certain sense, pull us out of our bodies, or the ways that smartphones enable us to disengage from the reality around us, or how our minds can be at the mercy of the stimuli around us, our struggles to pray shouldn't surprise us. As new ideas and conflicts emerge on our screens, we can enter into the reactive mind that Laird describes. By resisting the impulse to react, we can move toward what Laird describes as receptive mind. If reactive mind is like hardened soil that lacks rain or compost, receptive mind has been softened by the dew, rain, or nutrients of God's presence, gradually changing its ability to receive what is placed in it. Laird describes the fertility of this receptive state as "expanding inner stillness and spaciousness, intrinsic to awareness itself, which can now emerge more fully, due to the decluttering process of the practice of contemplation."[10]

If our minds and hearts remain hardened by the never-ending pressure of social media's never-ending content, and if our minds are constantly reacting to what we find on our digital devices, then we will struggle to receive what God freely gives us. At the very least, a routine time of reconnection with the ground of our being—a time away from distracting thoughts—can help us get a better sense of whether we are living in a state of reaction to the narratives around us or in a state of reception to the good things God hopes to do in our lives.

RESET YOURSELF REGULARLY

Early in my career as a writer, Lent was the first time I really reset myself and my use of digital technology. I made it part of my Lenten fast to only use social media on weekdays from nine to five. I had been told by a New York publishing executive that I needed to market my books on social media "until I dropped," so these boundaries felt like a kind of extreme sacrifice for my career at the time. For the first two or three weeks, I had to stop myself more often than I can count. Oftentimes I had my computer or phone right in front of me, and I would tap or click on a social media site, then close it rapidly as I remembered my fast. However, by the midpoint of Lent, I began to enjoy reading books on weekday evenings rather than pining after social media. I didn't even think about it over the weekends.

In his books *Deep Work* and *Digital Minimalism*, productivity expert Cal Newport rightly worries that a weekend off
social media could be followed by bingeing during the week.
Since Newport is concerned with productivity, limiting social
media use between the nine-to-five weekday hours may appear
especially bad in his eyes! While I personally removed all social
media apps from my smartphone and use a blocking app on
my web browser to limit my social media use each day, there
is value in setting limits that appear personally viable and offer
a taste of disengagement from social media and from constant
smartphone access. A forty-day social media fast for Lent has
become a common practice among many Christians because
it offers the benefit of doing something hard with the support
of Christian community—although the downside may include
losing touch with distant friends whom we message via social
media or those who are sick or housebound who rely on social media, so plan around that carefully. A set time of disengagement is vitally important to get a sense of how your spirit,
mind, and body feel after you have had some time in silence
away from technology and social media. In addition to Lent, I
now try to avoid social media each evening and weekend.

Since I have often misused technology to escape reality when
I'm anxious or busy, a regular time away from social media and
my smartphone helps me establish a baseline for personal and
spiritual health. I am much better at recognizing when I've
been stretched too thin because I'm not spending each day under the influence of social media's steady drip of disconnection
from my emotions or reactive thoughts.

Silence, solitude, and a singular focus are hard to find in
a technology-saturated world, but even before digital technology became pervasive, Howard Thurman noted the urgency of

finding solitude and silence away from the pressures of life. He wrote, "We must find sources of strength and renewal for our own spirits, lest we perish. There is a widespread recognition of the need for refreshment of the mind and the heart. . . . First, we must learn to be quiet, to settle down in one spot for a spell. Sometime during each day, everything should stop and the art of being still must be practiced."[11] These days, this time for a reset or renewal has often been replaced by using a smartphone. Mind you, I often appear a bit odd while sitting in a waiting room or at a café table with nothing in my hands—just sitting there. It's unusual to actively disengage from everything, but if you can retrain yourself to leave your phone out of sight and to enjoy a little silence without digital stimulation each day, you may find that these times offer mental and spiritual renewal.

Resetting ourselves in silence is a longtime spiritual practice that the desert fathers and mothers placed at the heart of their daily disciplines. While they routinely welcomed visitors and wrote letters to support local churches, they frequently praised the role of silence in spiritual formation. Syrian monk Isaac of Nineveh shared, "If you love truth, be a lover of silence. Silence like the sunlight will illuminate you in God and will deliver you from the phantoms of ignorance. Silence will unite you to God himself."[12]

The silence and stability of contemplation delivers us from the draining influence of digital technology. Rather than leaving us isolated or irrelevant, it can offer us the resources we need each day. Thomas Merton outlined the stakes of silent prayer and contemplation in the following way: "To praise the contemplative life is not to reject every other form of life, but to seek a solid foundation for every other human striving. Without the silence and recollection of the interior life, man loses contact with his real sources of energy, clarity, and peace."[13]

With a new baseline for spiritual formation in our lives, we'll be prepared to consider lasting changes that can limit the impact of digital formation while allowing spiritual formation to flourish. While we have access to life-giving spiritual practices that can help us reconnect with God and with each other, we need to make sure they become integrated into our lives. They'll never be as easy to practice or as immediately gratifying as social media or smartphones, so we need to consider ways to order our lives around the priority of spiritual formation.

... INVITATION TO RECONNECT ....

What is your reaction to the idea of silence or solitude? Prayerfully consider why you have that kind of relationship with silence and solitude.

Choose one of the digital detox options discussed in this chapter and set a time to test it out. Here are a few ideas to consider:

- Fast from your phone (except for answering calls, of course) and social media after dinner each evening.

- Remove social media completely from your smartphone for a month.

- For the next week, practice leaving your phone behind or at least in the glove box of your car when you go out.

- Fast completely from all social media for one or two days each week for a month, or choose a week- or month-long fast.

Even a weekend off social media is a great start. If you delete social media apps from your phone, you can always add them back. I encourage you: Don't turn the page until you have a detox plan of some sort in your schedule.

It does seem to be a luxury to be able to give thought and time to the ups and downs of one's private journey while the world around is so sick and weary and desperate. But, our Father, we cannot get through to the great anxieties that surround us until, somehow, a path is found through the little anxieties that beset us.

—HOWARD THURMAN

SEVEN

Get a Habit . . .
Like Monks and Nuns

Perhaps we can't help focusing on what monks and nuns give up when they enter religious life and take vows of poverty, chastity, and stability—the latter is a choice to remain in one place. For instance, a reporter from *The Oregonian* asked the monks from the Mount Angel Abbey what they gave up to join the monastery, what they missed, whether they felt lonely, and whether they ever had fun. From one monk to another, they had all given up careers that they didn't miss and possessions that they no longer required, although they could all stand to eat a bit more pizza. Whether they enjoyed the solitude of monastic life or found community among their fellow monks, loneliness wasn't an issue. *But do monks have fun?* One monk, surprised that the question even needed to be asked, simply replied, "Yes. I have fun."[1]

Regardless, each of the monks interviewed shared a deep contentment with the simplicity of their lives, the boundaries of daily schedules, and the freedom they had to pray five set times each day. We shouldn't confuse ourselves by thinking of the lives of monks and nuns as romantic or simple. It can be quite exhausting and even busy at times.[2] However, each of the monks interviewed by *The Oregonian* indicated that they were content with the freedom granted through their limitations.

In an interview with the sisters of the Summit Convent in New Jersey, sister Mary Catharine noted that she had seen increased interest from young women who long for the simplicity of monastic life. "With all the technology, I think they're just saturated," she shared. "And they see this life as really radical and they have a desire for it." And while there are many reasons to pursue a holy calling of contemplative prayer and work, she was quick to add, "If God is calling, you can't be happy doing anything else."[3] While the sisters miss out on the luxury of sleeping in on the weekends, they have a joy for life and a vibrant love for God that inspired photographer Toni Greaves to dedicate seven years to living in the convent's tiny guest quarters in order to write a book called *Radical Love* about the Summit's Sister Maria Teresa.

Regardless of what these monks and nuns gave up for the sake of their callings, the simplicity of their lives and the daily habit of prayer freed them for what was most important and gave them peace and contentment to enjoy God's love.

SOUL CARE FIRST

A few years ago, after facing the way that unhealthy habits can take root and how hard it is to choose the health of my soul, I wrote a rather honest blog post with the title "Do You Want to Be Made Well? Probably Not." I liked the *idea* of being healthy and centered in God, but changing my habits and choices was another matter. Making the health of our souls a priority requires intention, changes to our daily routines, and facing the ways our existing habits and routines may be harming us. Social media and smartphones are especially challenging because they can feel quite good in the moment, even if the accumulated impact on our souls is negative.

Oftentimes, soul care ends up pretty far down the list of priorities each day. Even at the start of the day many of us are more likely to check email or social media rather than grounding ourselves in God's loving presence. I have often felt this tug toward email or media right from the start of my day, as if I don't even have a choice between distraction or soul care. As the day begins to roll forward, I don't want to be at the mercy of my to-do list, current events, social media outrage, or the latest urgent message in my inbox. My hope is to be shaped and formed by God rather than by whatever I find on my phone first thing in the morning. Choosing silence isn't easy at the start of the day, and it doesn't get any easier. However, do we struggle in part with prioritizing soul care because we aren't sure which spiritual practices could be most beneficial, how they could help us, or how to fit them into our days?

I don't find it helpful to spend a lot of time discussing ways to block social media or limit smartphone use without also pointing to the alternative healthy practices we need and the benefits they offer. Rather than putting ourselves at the mercy of our digital devices, Christians can put their hope in God's loving presence, which offers us a solid, grounded space to stand as we enter our day. There is a world of difference between beginning the day trusting in God's presence and reacting to whatever flashes before us on our screens. By creating intentional space in our days, our souls can be nourished and supported by the Holy Spirit rather than allowing ourselves to be dragged this way and that by distracting messages, emotionally charged news reports, and never-ending social media updates. Each of us can recognize what will be most beneficial and life-giving for our souls as we make space for spiritual practices such as silence, meditation on Scripture, or a guided examination that leads to prayer. The challenge is that soul care has a long-term, cumulative effect on our lives that is hard to recognize in the short term. Our motivation for soul care is more likely to increase if we stick with spiritual practices that offer a contrast to the distractions of social media. In the meantime, the starting point for soul care needs to be as concrete, accessible, and specific as possible if it's going to overcome the easier digital habits already in our lives.

I don't think I would last very long in my opposition to digital formation if I didn't have a clear path toward spiritual practices and the freedom and peace God offers. In fact, digital formation derives so much of its power from our unintentional, even unthinking, use. If we are just passing time or disconnecting from a stressful moment, we aren't really addressing the deeper needs of our souls and are missing out on better ways to spend our time. In addition, digital devices and social media apps appear to be good for our relationships, are easy to use, and can even feel productive for our work. If we aren't oriented around something better, digital formation will win hands down.

What would it look like to put soul care ahead of every other priority in your day?

For me, it looks like dedicated time for silence, whether sitting, walking, or running, and praying *The Divine Hours* each day—a collection of Scripture readings and prayers arranged for set times: morning, afternoon, evening, and nighttime. When I plan my day, I make sure there's at least some time for silence before God—even if it ends up being part of a run or a trip in the car. Before the birth of our third child, I typically set aside some time to pray during our boys' quiet time each afternoon. Ideally, I also make space for some spiritual reading, but that can often hinge on naps and children's bedtimes these days. However, even a few minutes of reading in bed before the book falls on my face is better than nothing!

The key to making space for prayer and other spiritual formation practices is to pick a set time to make a specific practice happen. This doesn't have to be a major revolutionary goal. I trained myself to sit in silence before God by starting with five-minute sessions each evening. From my morning runs, which began as brisk walks, to praying the hours before work, there are intentional and specific spots in my day for soul care, such as, "When I sit down to work, I will pray *The Divine Hours* first." Having that priority of soul care at that point in my day means I now feel a bit lost if I forget my prayer book.

God desires to shape you into someone who is at peace in God's love and presence. That formation can be lost if we allow other things to crowd out our attention to God and the care God desires to bring to our souls. Soul care is easy to neglect because we are surrounded by urgent notifications and tasks. Our schedules can fill up, and our smartphones and other media devices can absorb uncounted hours each week. Without regular reflection, such as a daily Examen practice or daily journaling, I can neglect spiritual practices and soul care, letting the small anxieties and distractions of life add up. Over time, they will take their toll if left unchecked. One of the most effective ways to make soul care stick over time while resisting digital distraction is to learn a lesson from monks and nuns about forming regular habits in our lives.

GET A HABIT

"So you're watching the monks again?"

The ringing bells always tip off my wife when I'm watching the long and somewhat repetitive documentary *Into Great Silence*. This two-hour documentary following the daily routines of Carthusian monks in France features very little noise, save for shuffling feet on the stone floors, a monk who makes goofy noises for the monastery's cats, and the bells that signal a time for prayer. The call to prayer scenes are about as unspectacular as you can imagine. A solitary figure tugs on the rope to the bell tower while the monks file into the chapel. Soon enough, they begin chanting. Then, more work, more bells, more prayers, a meal, more work, and the occasional haircut with clippers. This isn't high drama, but it is the place where we can learn about a thriving prayer practice that is disconnected from almost all digital technology. Most importantly, these monks have a habit— well, technically two habits: the one they wear and the prayers that are prompted with the cue of ringing bells and preserved in their daily schedule and routines.

Monks and nuns usually aren't the first people we consider for an example of healthy technology use, since the only phones they may use, if at all, are communal monastery phones. I can't think of any social media workshops led by a monk or nun in a monastery off the top of my head. However, they can remind us what it feels like to work and pray in a state of disconnection from social media and digital devices. They have a handle on several valuable assets for us as we seek to reconnect with God in prayer. Monks and nuns can teach us a lot about developing good habits for spiritual formation, can model single-minded attentiveness, and can even remind us what it's like to live a relatively unplugged daily life. Habits that lead to the fulfillment of meaningful goals are the real starting point for a healthy interaction with digital technology. When pairing habits with spiritual practices, we can develop an intentional contemplative resistance to digital technology's goal of forming us into dopamine-driven notification addicts who crave compulsive, constant quick hits of stimulation and affirmation. The stability and rootedness of habitual spiritual practices can ground us against the constant disruption of technology. If we hope to imitate the happy monk standing in the field at the start of this book, we might ask whether his daily habits have something to teach us.

If your goal is to step out of the chaos of digital distraction and to then ground yourself in your identity as a child of God, then your habits can help you get there. Oftentimes a struggle to pray isn't a commentary on a person's sinfulness. There's simply a lack of intentional planning of each day's priorities and a neglect of long-term habit formation. Prayer needs a set place in your life in order to stick. Just as you are nourished by sitting down for three planned meals each day, you can also become spiritually nourished by praying for three set times each day. This is a simple habit to develop that has endured in the church for centuries.

Although a habit-inspired "capsule wardrobe" of interchangeable habits, hoods, and belts isn't a bad idea for ultraminimalist fashion if you ask me, the most instructive behavioral habits can be learned from the focused structure of a monk or nun's day. Most monastic orders integrate work and prayer into their days. Very few are fully devoted to prayer and silence like the Carthusians, and even they have to manage tasks such as chopping firewood, growing food in the garden, and maintaining their buildings. A convent down the road from our former home in Vermont sold some pretty spectacular cheesecakes, which sounds like just about the holiest thing you can make if you ask me.

Most importantly, our digital devices and social media are already cultivating habits in our lives. They have worn a series of patterns into our brains that govern our behavior each day. Resisting the habits of technology can be exhausting, as our willpower can be worn out like a muscle.[4] Bad habits can take hold faster than we'd like to admit, and replacing them with good habits will be a heavy lift at first. However, with a bit of planning and intention, habits become easier to integrate into our lives the longer we work at them. As noted earlier, while habit expert and Stanford psychologist B. J. Fogg trained some of the most profitable members of Silicon Valley's engineers and executives in "persuasive design" technology that used human psychological hacks to make apps and devices hard to put down, his basic approach to habit formation can help undo some of the harm he has done. According to Fogg, habits take shape when motivation, ability, and prompts converge.

Prompts to use technology or to do anything else can be self-imposed. For instance, when I wake up, I turn off the alarm on my phone, and most often my next step is to check my email, since the phone is already in my hand. If I'm waking up at five or six in the morning, it's absurd to think that I'll do anything useful with my email. It's just a habit. Turning off my alarm is the prompt. However, I also prompt myself to run by leaving my running clothes and shoes out so I can easily put them on in the morning. Making them easy to find and then put on means I can start running right away. Not dying of heart disease is one of my stronger motivations—although stress relief and mental space are also significant sources of motivation for running.

What could a healthy spiritual habit look like for you today? Perhaps think of how to replace the compulsion to check social media or email first thing in the morning. If email is too irresistible, consider subscribing to a daily email that offers spiritual reading each morning, such as the daily email from the Center for Action and Contemplation. If your smartphone is tough to resist at night, consider a different bedtime reading routine that doesn't include your phone, and use an alarm clock instead. If using your phone during the day is challenging, try prioritizing something positive, like sitting with a cup of coffee or iced tea in silence after lunch or during a point in the day when you know you'll have a little time to yourself. If you need an easier on-ramp for spiritual practices while using your phone, the Examen, which offers a time of reflection on the day and on where God may be present, can prove ideal. It's even available as an app, which is how I started practicing it (see apps like Reimagining the Examen or the Examine App).

A habit is most likely to take root if you have the right kind of prompt in place, an unmistakable cue that makes it obvious what comes next. For instance, I aim to stay off social media after five o'clock so I can read a book in the evening if I have any downtime (which hasn't been often since the birth of our third kid!). It helped to kick off this habit by picking up a few books that I was especially interested in reading. That made reading a book in the evening more desirable and helped the habit stick. I wasn't necessarily depriving myself of something, even if I was trying to avoid my phone and social media. I was making space for something healthy and beneficial. If staying off your phone altogether feels like too much of a stretch, consider deleting all social media apps from your smartphone and replacing them with apps that prompt deeper reflection and concentration. While I believe a long-term goal for most of us should be to use our phones less and be more involved with our neighbors, exchanging distracting apps for spiritually useful ones can help us transition toward more regular spiritual habits away from our phones.

I encourage you to pick any kind of simple starting point that will help you put some spiritual practices in place as easily and immediately as possible. Your work is cut out for you, but it's not impossible, and you can make it easy to start. In fact, as you begin to get a handle on what works and what doesn't work for resisting digital distraction and prioritizing spiritual reconnection with God, you'll begin to recognize when and where to set boundaries in your life.

ADD BOUNDARIES WHEN STRONG

Habits are essential for resisting digital distraction and preserving space to reconnect with God because it becomes harder to make good choices as our days wear us down. I don't make good decisions when I'm tired or stressed. That's when my self-destructive tendencies, like sloth, emerge. While healthy habits can keep us on track even when life is draining or stressful, at a certain point we may understandably run off the rails. From a challenging day at work to family drama to health challenges to disturbing current events, stress and exhaustion can leave us vulnerable, worn out, and more likely to make destructive choices. There is no doubt that spiritual perspectives must be considered in a difficult season. I have received prayer for deliverance and healing from anxiety that has proven extremely timely and restorative. Without undercutting the importance of prayer, the day-to-day reality of many Christians is that we can receive prayer in the midst of truly challenging and exhausting circumstances and still face some of the same struggles and temptations. Did prayer fail us?

I have found that oftentimes I need to consider my unhealthy patterns in a time of clarity and health in order to put helpful boundaries in place. In other words, I can figure out how to remove myself from sources of distraction, anxiety, and anger before I'm weak and worn down. I can recognize the patterns in my life that signal I'm overwhelmed or struggling and then set boundaries to protect myself. Within these boundaries I'll remain free to make better choices for the health of my soul and for my interactions with others. This is why I aim to prioritize time for silence and reflection in the afternoon, even a short time, simply to get a sense of my soul and to consider if I need more silence and prayer.

The principle here is a bit of a modernized take on the solitude of the desert fathers and mothers. Bear with me for a moment. Consider that Henri Nouwen advises us to "fashion our own desert where we can withdraw every day, shake off our compulsions, and dwell in the gentle healing presence of our Lord."[5] Perhaps one way to shake off our compulsions and the pull of distraction in a time of weakness is to set up blocks and limitations on our use of digital devices and apps. We could use blocking apps, delete distracting apps from our smartphones, or use timers to track our usage to better preserve the space we need, especially when life grows difficult and we may be more inclined to overuse or misuse our devices and apps. If we hope to remain grounded in God's love and mercy for our sake and for the sake of others, then we need to recognize when and how we need to withdraw from the disruption and fragmentation of technology and social media. This withdrawal is ultimately for the sake of others. As Thomas Merton wrote about the third- and fourth-century desert fathers and mothers, "They knew that they were helpless to do any good for others as long as they floundered about in the wreckage. But once they got a foothold on solid ground, things were different. Then they had not only the power but even the obligation to pull the whole world to safety after them."[6]

If soul care is our priority, and if we set up habits in order to make soul care a reality, then boundaries at key points in our days will help us preserve the healthy practices we've set in place. Removing distractions and temptations by setting boundaries for the day (or week) in a time of strength and reflection ensures that we aren't at the mercy of our emotions or the messages on our screens. Knowing when to withdraw, whether for a short time or several days, gives us greater control and freedom each day. Most importantly, we don't have to miss out on the benefits of connecting over social media if we place healthy boundaries around our apps and use them with more intention.

Any boundaries we place around ourselves to preserve our souls and our life-giving habits aren't just for our own sakes. They are for the benefit of others. Just as Rowan Williams presented contemplation as a spiritual practice that serves the world, so the boundaries and limits we set should help us remain grounded in the love of God that guides and empowers us to have more compassion and love for others. While prioritizing soul care and spiritual habits over the pull of digital formation may feel like an intervention that calls for significant personal reflection at first, the long-term fruit will help us bless others with fewer distractions and hindrances. In fact, once we've had this time of intervention, we may be ready to reconsider the correct place for technology in our lives.

WHAT WILL BE DIFFERENT TOMORROW?

As we near the end of this journey through digital formation and spiritual formation, I want to invite you into a kind of final scene where much of this journey's conflict is resolved and builds up to a final moment of reflection. While we still have some practical matters to address in the last chapter about healthy alternatives to digital technology, this is our moment of integration, where we bring all the main characters from previous scenes onstage for a resolution. If this book were a musical comedy (a big stretch here, folks, but stick with me), this would be the final number where all the main characters parade onto the street in their finest clothes and sing in the warm glow of the sun that sparkles on the fountain in the town square and offers vibrant life to the flowers lining main street. Everyone has passed through the conflict of the story, considered a new path forward, and is ready to face a new day. Life will be different because of what they've learned and experienced. Hope radiates as they embrace in the waning notes of their song.

But what will be different for you and for me tomorrow morning?

Part of our struggle with digital distractions is that they feel almost inevitable and irresistible. We know they affect us in negative ways, but we feel bound to them. Even if we know what's good for us and we train ourselves to develop good habits, most apps and devices aren't designed to be used in moderation. They're designed for bingeing and compulsive use. Can we sing and dance about a bright hope of joy and peace in God's presence today if the dark clouds of digital technology and social media apps appear to be looming on the horizon? It's insightful to learn about the dark side of social media and the benefits of spiritual formation, but how can we be sure we'll continue to reconnect with God and resist the fragmenting distractions of digital devices and social media?

I don't think all is lost, but I do think we need a very different mind-set moving forward if our cheerful optimism is going to have a chance. Even if we can make long lists of the benefits of social media and smartphones in our lives, we can no longer view them as allies or impartial tools. They are designed to become integral parts of our lives that we depend on at all costs, even to the point of making us feel that we have no choice but to use them. Our response must be informed and intentional.

If we place the health of our souls first and cultivate habits and boundaries, we can carefully watch how digital technology forms us in contrast to the results of spirituality. I personally have no intention of giving up on digital devices or social media altogether, but I can't see myself ever returning to a time when I don't have stringent blocks and limitations on my usage. I name my specific strategies in the resources section "A Starter Guide for Digital Boundaries" in the back of this book, but the foundational issue is to prioritize the health of our souls so that we can be present for God and for others and can take steps and form habits to make that possible.

To put on my parenting hat for a moment, our smartphones and social media apps have treated us quite badly; they need a lengthy time out; and as things stand, their creators have not yet earned our trust. Personal restrictions are essential since, as of this writing, their makers have not made significant strides in addressing the damage they have done to society and continue to inflict on it. While social media and technology continue to loom over our toe-tapping dance scene at the end of our journey, the good news is that we have the power to do one thing that no engineer or wily psychologist can ever prevent us from doing: turn our devices off.

We can choose to turn off our phones, obliterate notifications, delete social media apps, block the Facebook news feed, manage our postings or notifications through third-party apps, switch our screens to gray scale, block websites or the entire Internet for set stretches, or turn off our wireless routers. For all the ways that social media engineers and psychologists have worked to eliminate our perception of freedom and choice, we actually have plenty of ways to send away the looming threat of social media and technology. Our celebration and awareness of God's transforming love doesn't have to be crashed by distracting devices. It's not easy, but it's well within our reach.

The primary thing that holds many of us back is a fear of being disconnected from the people we love, the friends we admire, the colleagues who make us more effective, and the networks of information and media that make us informed, relevant, and entertained. We fear that we stand to lose so much if we start blocking social media or turn off the devices that have convinced us, in roughly a decade, that they are all but essential for human existence.

Implementing wide, sweeping blocks and boundaries on my social media and digital device use has freed up significant time for spiritual practices, personal hobbies, and the relationships that are most important to me. I've found quieter ways to maintain relationships beyond the roar of social media, and my perception is that I've lost no one close to me because of these restrictions. If anything, I've saved some of my most import-ant relationships by withdrawing from potential online con-flict and conserving more energy for my family, my in-person community, and distant friends whom I can reach with more personal and direct means.

Since social media is so easy to misuse and since we live in fear of being disconnected and left adrift in loneliness and so-cial isolation, I want to leave you with some ideas of how to use it differently and how to reconnect with God and with others in ways that either reimagine or avoid the traps of social media. This is hardly a comprehensive or one-size-fits-all program for social media use or avoidance. These are some hopeful possibil-ities for what could be different for you and for me when we wake up tomorrow morning. This is the place where I hope to leave you when the happy music fades. God's loving presence is here for you, but the space you create for God will determine whether the dark clouds of digital formation will overtake you or whether you will move forward with intention and purpose toward the spiritual abundance God intends for all.

. . . INVITATION TO RECONNECT . . . .

How can you make yourself more motivated to pray?

For example, set a date for a silent retreat and practice silent prayer leading up to it, or consider the history of Christians who prayed and found peace in God's loving presence.

How can you make it easier to pray?

For example, read a book like *Open Mind, Open Heart* or *Into the Silent Land* to learn the basics of contemplative prayer. Or con-sider ways to change your schedule to make time for prayer.

How can you prompt yourself to pray?

For example, after getting dressed each morning, I will sit in silence for ten minutes; when I drive to work, I will sit in silence before God; or I will sit in silence before lunch each day.

Our truest response to the irrationality of the world is to paint or sing or write, for only in such response do we find truth.

—MADELEINE L'ENGLE

EIGHT

Reconnect with
the Good and Beautiful

The typical Examen practice includes an awareness of God's presence in your day, gratitude for the events of the past day, and prayerful awareness of God's presence in today's challenges, as well as your concerns about tomorrow.

When we added a child-appropriate Examen to evening prayer with our kids, they expressed gratitude for watching television at the hotel—one month ago, two months ago, and so on. Television came up every night before anything. We don't own a television, so watching television on a big screen is a big deal for them. However, this time of self-reflection and prayerful gratitude and prayer really ran off the rails when they began expressing a fervent desire for God to bring dinosaurs back to life . . . and to give these dinosaurs the ability to speak. I can only trace this back to their watching *Lego Jurassic World* at a friend's house. As we ventured further from the concept of gratitude, let alone reality, they fleshed out the details of this prayer request. They added that they wanted God to also make these dinosaurs nice. I mean, why not swing for the fences at that point? When a friend learned about their prayer for dinosaurs, she warned them that dinosaurs aren't nice. Always ready with an answer for the hope within them, one of my boys countered, "That's how prayer works!"

While the daily Examen and prayer time with our boys isn't quite having the desired effect yet for anyone involved (those dinosaurs haven't shown up yet), we are at least beginning to discuss the importance of practicing gratitude each day. A daily practice of gratitude helps us see what we have with greater clarity and offers us a helpful alternative to the daily temptations of comparison and envy on social media. I incorporate gratitude into my daily Examen practice, which at bare minimum reflects on a point of encouragement, a point of discouragement, and then looks ahead to the coming day with prayer and trust in God. At the very least it's a nice alternative to our advertisement-driven consumer economy that pounces on our discontent and desire for more by reminding us of everything we *don't* have or *desperately* need. We can begin countering this invasion of our minds and our time by making space for daily practices that help us care for our souls, remain grounded in the present moment, and use our time well for God and for others.

You could say that Christians, guided by love of God and love of neighbor, can counter our digital, ad-driven consumer culture with an alternative Christian subculture that encourages simplicity, gratitude, and awareness of others. Unfortunately, there's not a lot of money for people who spend their time encouraging folks to pray in silence, to keep a gratitude journal, to walk in the woods, to make art, to creatively meet the needs of our communities, or to spend more time with people in person rather than scrolling through status updates online. If advertisers, engineers, and psychologists aim to make their devices and apps irresistible, then how can we reclaim the freedom of our attention and exercise the ability to see the goodness and beauty around us each day?

As a starting point, instead of focusing on the good things other people have on social media, consider how you can regularly express gratitude for what you have, sharing this either privately or on social media. Gratitude has been proven by sociologists to have positive effects on mental health and well-being.[1] Ann Voskamp's perennial bestseller *One Thousand Gifts* shares her life-changing story of embracing gratitude as a regular spiritual practice. Thankfulness is an essential element of personal and communal prayer and worship. We are exhorted in the Psalms to enter God's presence with songs of thanksgiving.

As we imagine our public use of social media and technology in the future, we could begin by asking how we can testify with thankfulness for God's presence in our lives, the blessings we're grateful to have, or the ways we have witnessed the love of God shine through others. Perhaps our souls and the souls of others would be most encouraged if we prioritized gratefully sharing how God has shown up in our lives each day or the things that make us come alive. Living in greater awareness of the beauty and truth we've experienced will make us more prepared to pray simply because we'll be aware of what God has given us.

Mind you, that isn't to say we should only share about spiritual topics. Rather, gratitude helps us beware the social media tendencies of viewing others with envy or sharing about the latest outrage in the news, scandal, or poorly worded tweet. We will surely wear ourselves out if we only focus on what's wrong in the world, and we can rest assured that plenty of people are counting on gaining attention by being outrageous or cruel in their words or deeds. No one benefits if we primarily fixate on the latest outrage each day—and we may well drain ourselves of valuable energy and focus for the activism or advocacy that truly can make a difference in our community!

RECONNECT PERSONALLY, NOT GENERALLY

My small group leader from eight years ago was the first person I knew who intentionally avoided Facebook. He was firm in his convictions about abstaining, and he explained it to me like this: "If I really want to get connected with people, I'll send a text about meeting for coffee or call them up."

He had a point.

As grateful as I am to know what's going on with my friends, family, and colleagues through their social media updates, the social media connections that are most personal and intimate are usually maintained through the occasional private message or discussions in small private groups. More often than not, the digital interactions that mean the most to me tend to occur via email, text message, or a voicemail via the Voxer app. These are direct and personal interactions where we mutually value each other by specifically reaching out.

Social media has a way of creating uneven connections between people. Someone may aspire to connect with a favorite author, a celebrity, or someone who is perceived as smart, popular, or creative. We may want to be friends with people who are most likely at their limit for personal social connections and who may receive similar requests all the time. As a relatively unknown author, I have felt overwhelmed by the sheer number of connections I have on social media and the number of friend requests from strangers that never seem to stop coming. From the standpoint of managing human relationships, thousands of connections are simply impossible to maintain. I may be loosely connected with thousands of people on social media. The sad part is that I may fail to have deeper interactions with the people closest to me if I'm too preoccupied with a kind of surveillance friendship on social media. Surveillance friendship doesn't have the capacity for bearing burdens in the presence of others, even if social media does make it easier to share funds with those in a time of crisis. If social media consumes hours of my time each week, I may not be aware of or have the time to help members of my community who may be stretched to the limit. It's no mistake that my blocks and boundaries on social media coincided with more time devoted to serving in my church and community.

As I've added more blocks to social media, I've made an effort to open more avenues of direct communication with a manageable number of friends. Even making one or two connections via a text message or a three- to four-minute voicemail on Voxer each week can leave me feeling more in touch with the people close to me rather than with my many weaker social media ties. While I'm not a great note writer, because I put a lot of pressure on myself to capture *everything* someone means to me in a three-sentence note, several friends have shared touching notes that have left me encouraged and more aware of how much our friendship means.

These personal connections are vital. I may think I know how someone is doing because of a series of social media posts, but is that really the case? Concerns about projecting a false image aside, there's only so much we may want to share on social media. Personal medical concerns, stress over work, or a challenging situation with a child will likely remain beneath the surface of social media posts. I'll often only find out about those issues if I reach out more directly and personally. I can only bear the burdens of others if I am willing to enter into their lives to find out about their pain, anxiety, or disappointments.

When we moved to a new town a few years ago, I wanted to make stronger connections with the families with children we started meeting. I picked one morning each week to host a playgroup. It started out somewhat ambitiously with a few friends and a lunch that we cooked and served around the table. As we invited more families, we simplified the food options, I strapped down the sandbox lid so we wouldn't find sand in our kids' beds, and chaos ensued on the rainy days when about fifteen kids bounced off the walls of our small ranch house. I'll be the first to tell you that this group played to a lot of my weaknesses. I like quiet and order and disliked dealing with the occasional times when the kids got out of hand. We had to clean and pick up the house, hide choking hazards, wipe peanut butter off the couch repeatedly, quarantine any prized Lego projects that our boys didn't want to see smashed, and then clean and pick up the house all over again. Despite the work and the challenging moments, it was well worth it to have that weekly time for in-person connection. As someone who works online, has family in a different time zone, and whose nearest colleagues require a two-hour drive that includes the lion's den of Nashville traffic, the sacrifices were worth it. A weekly in-person gathering was far and away the best thing I could have done to make deeper, personal connections in our town.

The greatest gift we can give someone isn't sharing their project on social media or affirming them with "likes" each time they post something. Our gift is our presence and complete attention—truly seeing people as they are and not as we imagine them or even, at times, as they present themselves. That presence may be as simple as giving a tired parent a cup of coffee or keeping my phone put away so I can focus on conversations during my church's coffee hour. We are saturated by weak connections and shallow brand communities centered around products and services. If we do spend time on social media, we will often see the most benefit from intentionally supplementing the stronger relationships that begin with in-person interactions.

RECONNECT WITH CREATIVITY

In 2017, I tried something radical that I never would have imagined doing: I bought an art journal and some charcoal pencils. Struggling with anxiety in the wake of the 2016 election and the endless flow of bad news and crises, I needed an activity that didn't involve anything digital. I had become so preoccupied with current events that I had lost a grip on my leisure time—although my work time suffered as well. It's so easy to put ourselves at the mercy of our media and digital devices that we may struggle to know how to use our leisure time without a screen leading the way. According to philosopher Jacques Ellul, "If you have to gather people together and lead them in order to show them what to do, everything is lost."[2] Feeling lost, I turned to art—more realistically, doodling.

Settling down at a table in one of our small town's cafes, I opened to a blank page and stared. As a writer with a pen in hand, the blank page is a welcome invitation to create. Holding a charcoal pencil in place of a pen left me at a complete loss. I ended up sketching the cover of a Thomas Merton book I'd been reading because I literally couldn't think of anything else. Over time, I began sketching the drawings from my kids' picture books. *Good Night, Good Night, Construction Site* resulted in some drawings that proved to be crowd pleasers, but it stretched the limits of my abilities. Finally, Mo Willems' series of Pigeon books hit the sweet spot of challenging my minimal artistic training while making it possible to create something that didn't look too awful. Each Sunday for about a year, I added another pigeon doodle to my collection. After passing the two-year mark of taking up my doodling hobby, I certainly haven't created any masterpieces, but it has provided an enjoyable, unplugged activity. On occasion, I've shared images of my doodles on social media, which have proven therapeutic for some parents familiar with the Pigeon "genre." I have since added pastels to the mix, but I haven't progressed past still life fruit yet.

Even more important for my mental health, gardening has become one of my primary and favorite creative outlets. I've enjoyed building the frames for raised beds, setting up a trellis for grapevines, and arranging beds of greens, kale, and even a mystery seed (sorry, kids, they're French radishes). One friend offered the ultimate compliment when our raised-bed garden at our former home was on the verge of harvest: "This garden design is a work of art!" Even planting a few pots of flowers on our front porch has proven immensely good for my soul and mental health, reminding me to create spaces of creative expression and beauty.

If battling the summer heat or living in an urban setting makes gardening unappealing or impossible, perhaps singing or playing an instrument could help you reconnect with creativity, as well as allow you to forge relationships with people who share your interests. Singing in a group can relieve stress and is one of the best activities for improved mental health. One study from Oxford found that creating music in a group is an excellent way to build community: "Group singing not only helps forge social bonds, it also does so particularly quickly, acting as an excellent icebreaker. We've also shown that community singing is effective for bonding large groups, making it an ideal behaviour to improve our broader social networks. This is particularly valuable in today's often alienating world, where many of our social interactions are conducted remotely via Facebook and Twitter."[3]

In addition to the experience of singing, music itself can counteract some of the harm done by digital devices and can counteract the sources of fear and pain in our lives—even physical pain. In an essay on the benefits of singing, one choir member shared an experience that my friends who sing in choirs have also confirmed with me:

> Music is awash with neurochemical rewards for working up the courage to sing. That rush, or "singer's high," comes in part through a surge of endorphins, which at the same time alleviate pain. When the voices of the singers surrounding me hit my ear, I'm bathed in dopamine, a neurotransmitter in the brain that is associated with feelings of pleasure and alertness. Music lowers cortisol, a chemical that signals levels of stress. Studies have found that people who listened to music before surgery were more relaxed and needed less anesthesia, and afterward they got by with smaller amounts of pain medication. Music also releases serotonin, a neurotransmitter associated with feelings of euphoria and contentment. "Every week when I go to rehearsal," a choral friend told me, "I'm dead tired and don't think I'll make it until 9:30. But then something magic happens and I revive . . . it happens almost every time."[4]

While I doubt that spending an hour on social media each day will help me or anyone else all that much, there are many reasons to pursue activities that foster in-person community, allow us to express ourselves creatively, or give us the satisfaction of completing something challenging that stretches us to the edges of our abilities. It can be especially helpful to create something we can see in its final form so that we can celebrate what we have made.

While witnessing the transition from low-tech living at his monastery to high-tech farming and production, Thomas Merton looked to the practical craftsmanship of the Shaker communities in America as an alternative view of production and craft. Minimal digital technology and craftsmanship offer space both for personal restoration and for spiritual renewal. Philip Thompson writes: "Merton believed we could restore our true selves amidst the diminishments of the technological world. The restoration would include sane forms of work, appropriate small-scale technologies, the encouraging of crafts, a tapping into the restorative possibilities of nature, and learning the lessons of the solitary. If we pursued these possibilities with wisdom, we could recover our connection to a divine reality and promote a new balance in our lives."[5]

Along the same lines as Merton, Cal Newport, who is a professor of computer science, praises the value of craftsmanship and artistic hobbies as a response to digital distractions in his book *Digital Minimalism*. Whether we do so for a career or as a leisure activity, we will find a great deal of joy and freedom when we can make something—just about anything—rather than seeking to define ourselves based on online feedback or interaction.

I countered my anxiety about becoming a first-time parent by building a side crib, following a friend's plans, of course, that was sturdy enough to continue using for the rest of our children. I can't draw a straight line between my anxiety about parenting versus the restoration that came through creating that side crib. It simply offered a variety of "treatments" for my overactive mind by stretching my limited woodworking abilities, providing a concrete way to helpfully prepare for the baby, and allowing my mind to be present for God while I worked. Upon completion, I had a visible accomplishment that I could be proud of each time I stepped into our bedroom. It was certainly more helpful than the time I walked up and down the steps with a ten-pound weight cradled in my arms so I could practice not dropping the baby. As proud as I was of my side crib project (I won't go into detail about the wobbly storage shelves project), a family in Vermont may offer the most striking alternative lifestyle to counter digital formation by fostering a largely unplugged lifestyle.

Robin MacArthur and her husband Tyler Gibbons form the folk band Red Heart the Ticker. Robin is also a novelist. She and Tyler live on a large patch of family land up in the mountains of Vermont. I visited their farm while working on an article about them for *Vermont Magazine*. They live in a cabin they built themselves, room by room. Tyler told stories about where the kitchen sink and countertops came from, and he could go on about the process of adding a second story by himself! Just a short stroll down their dirt road, we sat down to talk in the spacious cabin owned by Robin's extended family. The walls in the living room were lined with instruments, many of which family members had built themselves. On many evenings the whole family gathered together in the spacious room to play folk songs together.

At the time of our interview, Robin and Tyler had recorded several of their songs on the property in various barns and rooms that added familiar sounds to the background of the recordings. Robin's grandmother spent her last days in the room that is now their studio, quietly singing the songs from their last album. While you can find Red Heart the Ticker on social media and on digital music sites, as well as online updates about Robin's novel, I continue to reflect on their creative life that appears alternative, even extreme, to us today. Should it be the alternative? At the very least, perhaps it shouldn't be such a dramatic outlier. As much as I feel intimidated by the thought of building a house by myself in the wilds of the Vermont wilderness, there are elements of the ways this family builds things, gathers for music, and maintains a measure of solitude that could be deeply restorative for people who feel overwhelmed by the force of digital formation.

If we can't find time to create things apart from our digital devices, are we in danger of placing ourselves at the mercy of our consumer economy and the digital ecosystem? At the very least, nondigital hobbies and activities offer our minds valuable space for examination and reflection while we work.

RECONNECT WITH BLESSINGS

There are so many forces using technology and social media to pull us apart, to sell us things, and to generate emotional responses, it's hard to know where to start sometimes. As complicated as this problem is, our way forward can begin with some simple steps. Besides turning the phone off and putting it out of sight, we can begin to make space for spiritual formation by making small, steady changes.

Let's return to our question: What will be different tomorrow morning? We could give ourselves the simple goal to pass along a blessing or encouragement to someone else. Surely we know people who are discouraged, anxious, lonely, suffering, or fearful. We could show up for someone to bless them with our presence or help at a time of need. We could bring a welcome light to their day by sharing a brief message via a note, brief visit, phone call, text message, or email. Heck, we could even use social media to bless them if that sounds easier! Whatever you need to do to start out will work, provided it's personal. One simple, positive blessing or encouraging word takes only a few minutes and can disconnect us from the negativity and anger that can sweep us off our feet on social media. Perhaps it may sound more viable to set up a coffee meeting, phone call, or lunch once a month with someone who is important to you.

The Psalms are filled with laments, requests, and blessings, and we can take a page from the Psalms to speak blessings over people, to lament with them, or to pray on their behalf. While I'm sure an encouraging post or a blessing on a social media profile would be appreciated and an improvement over divisive posts, many need specific conversations that speak blessings over others, prayers for times of need, offers of concrete help, or affirmations of God's goodness in their lives. If technology isn't going away, then we can choose how we use it, to pass on blessings, encouragement, assistance, condolences, and affirming words. Whether or not we use technology, a simple practice of blessing others regularly offers a step toward using our time more intentionally and constructively. We may become more aware of the needs of others, pray for them more regularly, and exercise more caution and care when we do engage with social media and other forms of digital connection if we make blessing a daily habit.

That isn't to say that we avoid the hard conversations or step away from advocacy and demanding accountability from governments, businesses, or influential individuals. There most certainly is a place for that kind of activism and advocacy. However, do we skew toward an unhelpful negativity and outrage far more often than is healthy or helpful? What if your goal for the next week would be to bless someone in your network of friends or colleagues—whether through words or deeds? Perhaps you could make it your goal to use social media to intentionally promote worthwhile work that is overlooked, to thank those who have made the world a better place, or to honor good people who may go unnoticed and unrecognized.

Information overload in our digital networks is a real problem; encouragement overload is not. We don't have to retreat from the hard work of advocacy on behalf of those who are suffering to reimagine a more constructive, life-giving approach to our days, especially our use of social media and technology. As followers of Jesus, who became incarnate among humanity, personally touched those he healed, and sent his followers to testify about the life of God among them, Christians have every reason to prioritize physical presence among others, compassion for those who are suffering, and using our words to bless and guide others toward God's transformative presence and love. Jesus was personal and present in his approach to each day, and we may surrender too much if we uncritically live hours of each day through our online profiles and posts.

We are surrounded by people who may have real, pressing needs or personal battles weighing on their minds. If we reach out to them with a blessing, we may also learn about ways we can provide material support or a compassionate presence. Our blessings can extend beyond the words we share and take the form of the ministry described in Matthew 25: feeding the hungry, clothing those in need, welcoming the stranger, caring for the sick, and visiting the imprisoned.

Digital devices and social media can have their place at times, but the body and blood of our compassionate and fully present Savior remind us each Sunday that we need flesh-and-blood connection. The God who is always present for us desires to reconnect with us and to help us reconnect with others because there is something better to be found in the tears, sweat, blisters, and blood of the people right around us. We can't tap or swipe to make their pain disappear. We can't share about their pain on social media and delude ourselves into thinking we've helped them. God calls us to watch and pray alongside the weary, fearful world.

If we struggle with a lack of direction or feel aimless, losing ourselves in distraction and digital discovery, perhaps we can look around for the people who are going through trials, the ones who are desperately looking for someone to watch and pray with them. They may be looking for presence or may crave a blessing. They want us to look them in the eyes, to absorb their pain, and to bear it with them. In their hour of trial, we can help carry the weight of their burdens alongside them. We may also discover along the way that we are becoming truly free from the afflictions and distractions of our screens. We have learned that the God who is always present with us and who desires to reconnect with us has inspired us to reconnect with others, generously sharing God's loving presence with a suffering world.

...INVITATION TO RECONNECT ....

How has someone recently blessed you in a personal way?

How can you become more personally present to bless one person this week?

Test out one of the creative activities or projects mentioned in this book for a set period to see how it changes your emotional or spiritual state. For example, try doodling weekly for two months, join a choir for two months, take music lessons for six months, or over the next week, play music while making dinner.

Epilogue

If I could condense the message of this book into a simple mantra to reconnect, it could be this:

Protect your time.
Prioritize one-on-one interactions.
Restore your spirit with daily silence.

If you can make space for these three practices, you'll improve your awareness of the ways digital technology and other elements of your day are helping or harming you. Silence will make space for God, and one-on-one interactions with others can challenge you to look beyond the weaker, shallow connections of social media. Restoration is God's gift for us, but we must make a space for it.

A STARTER GUIDE
FOR DIGITAL BOUNDARIES

WHILE I HAVE already mentioned some of my ideas for placing boundaries around social media and technology to preserve spiritual formation, this is a more comprehensive list that offers a variety of options for consideration.

Some of these ideas are simple.

Some of these ideas are complicated.

Some of these ideas involve technology.

Some of these ideas involve everything short of tossing your phone in a pond.

If these ideas don't help, then consider the "pond toss" option.

REPLACE TECHNOLOGY

Depending on your struggles with social media or compulsive smartphone usage, consider trying at least one of these practices for at least a week, but thirty days is ideal:

- Read all news on a nonpartisan website or subscribe to a local paper rather than social media.

- Use a pocket calendar to manage your schedule.

- Keep your phone out of your bedroom when you are sleeping and use an alarm clock.

- Use a paper journal rather than a note-taking app.

- Write a simple thank you note to a friend or family member each week.

EASY PRACTICES FOR GUARDING CHOICE AND ATTENTION

These are simple, free, and easily reversible. Perhaps some of these steps may appear challenging at first, but I encourage you to try them. Try these practices for a day, a week, or a month; assess how you feel; then consider if you want to reverse any of these steps for a day, a week, or a month. There isn't a one-size-fits-all solution per se, but we did all manage to get along just fine before smartphones were everywhere, so these steps are worth a shot:

- Set up gray scale on your smartphone. (You'll find this under Settings → Accessibility on most phones.)

- Get rid of all app notifications on your smartphone. (You'll find this under Settings → Notifications on most phones.)

- Remove all social media apps from your smartphone. (Hold your finger down on the app icon on your screen, wait for it to wiggle, then tap on the *x* to delete it. You can add it again anytime from the app store.)

- Remove all games from your smartphone.

- Place all remaining distracting apps you want to keep in a folder called "Distractions."

- As a general rule, make your phone more boring and more useless in order to cut down on your usage.

MANAGE SOCIAL MEDIA IN THIRD-PARTY APPS

Buffer, Hootsuite, and Later all offer ways to manage social media sites without having to fully engage in the stream of social media feeds. I manage many of my social media postings through these apps rather than getting distracted by the sites or social media apps themselves.

DELETE, RELOAD, AND DELETE

I deleted Instagram from my phone, but when I needed to run an ad for an ebook promotion, I downloaded it again. I only use the app to set up an ad campaign, and when the campaign is set, I delete the app until I need it again.

APPS FOR SMARTPHONES AND TABLETS

- Freedom: Blocks the Internet completely (not on apps, though) on digital devices and computers. I schedule an Internet block from nine in the evening to five in the morning every day on my smartphone.

- Moment: Tracks smartphone usage and sends notifications throughout the day on my progress.

COMPUTER TOOLS

- StayFocusd: A lifesaver for using social media within limits. Specify which sites you want to use for a limited time, set the amount of time allowed each day on those sites, and select which days you want to use the blocks. As of this writing, I limit myself to a total of twenty minutes per day on Twitter, Facebook, and Instagram combined.

- Freedom: I set thirty-minute blocks for all websites while working on my computer.

- Tomighty Pomodoro timer: I typically set up twenty-five-minute stretches of work and then take five-minute breaks to read, take a brief stroll, or sit in silence.

- SelfControl 2: Set longer blocks for specific websites, including social media, news, or sports sites. I can still access the Internet for work, but my main temptations can be blocked for hours at a time.

- Kill News Feed: The Facebook news feed becomes a pleasant sea of white, while allowing you to see notifications, messages, and group or event postings.

- Ad Block Pro: Most websites ask to be whitelisted by this browser add-on, but it remains helpful to minimize the number of ads I see each day.

MAKE IT FEEL GOOD TO DO OTHER THINGS

I try to give myself simple rewards for my regular daily tasks. For instance, I try to read *The Divine Hours* right after pouring my coffee so that I can associate prayer with coffee at its hottest and best.

When it comes to work, a writing program called Scrivener lets me set up a daily writing goal and a project writing goal for each session. The little bar on the word count goal changes from red to orange to green as I complete the goal for each session. For a fifty-thousand-word book, I aim for at least four hundred words each day. It's an easy enough goal to hit in twenty-five minutes, a typical Pomodoro and Freedom session. Most importantly, it feels really good to move from the red bar to the green bar because it feels good to make the color red go away. That isn't much, but it's enough to make me want to block distractions and get to work. Of course the reward of writing a book is much, much better than seeing that green bar, but that green bar has become a simple reward for accomplishing my work each day.

At home I try to use reading in the evening as a reward for getting the dishes done rather than frittering time away on news sites, social media (which is usually blocked anyway), or hockey news sites. I often feel that I've missed out on something really important from my day if I go to bed without having read on the couch a little bit in the evening—as if I've immersed myself in work and household chores all day without a simple pleasure! *The horror!* I try to let that drive me to get my household tasks done faster without distraction from social media or my phone so that I can get that reading time on the couch or in bed.

Just make sure that the reward isn't *another* bad habit! A massive bowl of ice cream or a half hour of social media use before bedtime would defeat the purpose of having rewards!

A STARTER GUIDE
FOR SPIRITUAL PRACTICES

AT THE RISK of repeating what I've shared in my previous book, *Flee, Be Silent, Pray*, I want to offer a few practical starting points for making space for spiritual practices and the habits that can help them stick in your life. These aim to provide an accessible place to begin. Over time, it is always ideal to add more time and practices, as well as some kind of spiritual support or direction from other Christians.

CONSIDER HOW YOU WILL START YOUR DAY

What will your first steps be after you wake up?

Perhaps you could read a passage from the divine hours or just pick a single psalm or verse from the morning office. Another option is to choose a psalm ,or a verse from a psalm, and to sit with it for two minutes. Before prayer became a more regular habit, I used the Common Prayer app because it sends a regular reminder to pray.

I have used the Center for Action and Contemplation's daily email (via cac.org) as a jumping-off point for my day, especially since I have often turned to email immediately after waking up.

Others may prefer to begin the day with two to five minutes of silence (with the goal of twenty to thirty minutes eventually) or a time of silence while walking or running. If you forget to do this at home or are unable to, consider taking a few minutes of silence while commuting or running an errand.

CONSIDER A CHECK-IN PRACTICE

Whether praying the afternoon office, journaling, reading a spiritual book, or sitting in silence, consider a time in the middle of the day to check in and to reorient yourself. If it helps, make this enjoyable at first by starting a book you've been wanting to read or buying a coffee a few times until this check-in becomes a regular part of your day.

When my kids are at school or preschool, I have often benefited from twenty minutes of silent centering prayer in the middle of the day.

CONSIDER HOW TO END YOUR DAY

The Examen offers a time of reflection at the end of the day, asking where God was throughout each part of the day and focusing on a source of discouragement and encouragement. It resolves with an invitation to pray about something from the day and to look ahead in faith and trust toward tomorrow. I have often combined the Examen with journaling. Some also observe five minutes of silence after the Examen.

While you may choose to pray the evening office or the compline at the end of your day, this may be an ideal time to read a longer passage of Scripture or a spiritual book.

Whatever you choose, start small, and don't worry about missing it sometimes or doing it imperfectly. You will gradually develop strength for these spiritual practices, and the results will show themselves over time.

For more practical ideas about integrating spiritual practices into your life, I go into greater detail in my book *Flee, Be Silent, Pray: Ancient Prayers for Anxious Christians.*

RECOMMENDED READING

SPIRITUALITY

An Ocean of Light by Martin Laird
Into the Silent Land by Martin Laird
Conjectures of a Guilty Bystander by Thomas Merton
Returning to Reality by Philip M. Thompson
Centering Prayer and Inner Awakening by Cynthia Bourgeault
Essential Writings by Howard Thurman
The Rule of Benedict by Joan Chittister
Open Mind, Open Heart by Thomas Keating

TECHNOLOGY

Alone Together and *Reclaiming Conversation* by Sherry Turkle
Digital Minimalism by Cal Newport
How to Break Up with Your Phone by Catherine Price
Ten Arguments for Deleting Your Social Media Accounts Right Now by Jaron Lanier
iGen: Why Today's Super-Connected Kids Are Growing Up Less Rebellious, More Tolerant, Less Happy—and Completely Unprepared for Adulthood—and What That Means for the Rest of Us by Jean M. Twenge

ACKNOWLEDGMENTS

MY CHILDREN Ethan, Brennan, and Bethany gave me the greatest reasons to write this book. I didn't want my use of social media or digital technology to prevent me from being fully present for their joy, games, Lego creations, cardboard projects, laughter, and endless questions. This project started because I wanted to reconnect with them, but over time I also found a spiritual urgency and resolution to the fragmentation of digital technology. Sources of wisdom, encouragement, and guidance included Seth Haines, Marlena Graves, Matthew Bradley, Shawn Smucker, Andi Cumbo-Floyd, John and Alta Ludlam, Bradley Wright, Stephen Mizell, Anne Bogel, Dr. Michelle Panchuk, and countless other friends and colleagues who supported this project along the way.

My wife, Julie, carried our family through the big due dates, listened to extensive Merton monologues, reviewed especially tricky chapters, and helped carry many of my burdens while also bearing the weight of a university professor's teaching load. This was not an easy book to write, and she made it possible to accomplish while preserving my mental health.

This project took its current shape thanks to the guidance of my original editor, Valerie Weaver-Zercher, and Amy Gingerich of Herald Press. Valerie put significant thought and effort into guiding the structure and introduction of this book as well as into guiding the overall creative direction and titling process. The team at Herald Press, including Joe Questel, LeAnn Hamby, and Alyssa Bennett Smith, patiently worked through the planning of this book and my slow process. I am grateful for their graciousness throughout. Amy and Margot Starbuck took the final revisions to the next level, adding clarity, tolerating my jokes, and making the final book far more accessible for readers.

NOTES

Introduction

Thomas Merton, *Conjectures of a Guilty Bystander* (New York: Image Books, 1965), 128.

1   See Paul Quenon, *In Praise of the Useless Life: A Monk's Memoir* (Notre Dame, IN: Ave Maria Press, 2018).

2   Cal Newport, *Digital Minimalism: Choosing a Focused Life in a Noisy World* (New York: Penguin Random House, 2019), 6.

3   Andrew Perrin and Jingjing Jiang, "About a Quarter of U.S. Adults Say They Are 'Almost Constantly' Online," Pew Research Center, March 14, 2018, http://www.pewresearch.org/fact-tank/2018/03/14/about-a-quarter-of-americans-report-going-online-almost-constantly/.

4   See Aaron Smith, "Declining Majority of Online Adults Say the Internet Has Been Good for Society," Pew Research Center, April 30, 2018, http://www.pewinternet.org/2018/04/30/declining-majority-of-online-adults-say-the-internet-has-been-good-for-society/; and Janna Anderson and Lee Rainie, "The Future of Well-Being in a Tech-Saturated World," Pew Research Center, April 17, 2018, http://www.pewinternet.org/2018/04/17/the-future-of-well-being-in-a-tech-saturated-world/.

5   Yudhijit Bhattacherjee, "Smartphones Revolutionize Our Lives—but at What Cost?" *National Geographic*, January 25, 2019, https://www.nationalgeographic.com/science/2019/01/smartphones-revolutionize-our-lives-but-at-what-cost/.

6   Andrew Perrin and Madhu Kumar, "About Three-in-Ten U.S.

Adults Say They Are 'Almost Constantly' Online," Pew
Research Center, July 25, 2019, https://www.pewresearch.org/
fact-tank/2019/07/25/americans-going-online-almost-constantly/.
7 "Time Flies: U.S. Adults Now Spend Nearly Half a Day
Interacting with Media," Nielsen, July 31, 2018, https://www
.nielsen.com/us/en/insights/news/2018/time-flies-us-adults-now
-spend-nearly-half-a-day-interacting-with-media/; see also "Tech
Addiction by the Numbers," *PC Magazine*, June 11, 2018, https://
www.pcmag.com/article/361587/tech-addiction-by-the-numbers
-how-much-time-we-spend-online.
8 Adam Alter, *Irresistible: The Rise of Addictive Technology and the
Business of Keeping Us Hooked* (New York: Penguin, 2017), 13–14.
9 Catherine Shu, "We Finally Started Taking Screen Time
Seriously," *TechCrunch*, December 25, 2018, https://techcrunch
.com/2018/12/25/we-finally-started-taking-screen-time-seriously
-in-2018/.
10 Sullivan was an early adopter of blogging who posted at a furious
pace. See Katie Zavadski, "A Look Back at Andrew Sullivan's The
Dish," *New York Magazine*, February 22, 2015, http://nymag.com/
intelligencer/2015/02/andrew-sullivan-dish-highlights.html. Some
of Sullivan's writing since his blogging days has been controversial.
11 Andrew Sullivan, "I Used to Be a Human Being," *New York
Magazine*, September 2016, http://nymag.com/intelligencer/2016/
09/andrew-sullivan-my-distraction-sickness-and-yours.html.
12 Jacques Ellul, "New Hope for the Technological Society: An
Interview with Jacques Ellul," interview by Berta Sichel, *ETC: A
Review of General Semantics* 40, no. 2 (July 1, 1983): 192–95.
13 Jacques Ellul, "Note to the Reader," *The Technological Society*,
trans. John Wilkinson (New York: Alfred A. Knopf, 1967), xxv.
14 Ibid., 4.
15 "Spiritual Formation," Renovaré, accessed June 12, 2019,
https://renovare.org/about/ideas/spiritual-formation.
16 M. Robert Mulholland Jr., *Invitation to a Journey: A Road Map
for Spiritual Formation*, rev. and expanded (Downers Grove, IL: IVP,
2016), 19–30.
17 Howard Thurman, *Essential Writings* (New York: Orbis Books,
2006), 60.
18 Cynthia Bourgeault, *Centering Prayer and Inner Awakening*

(Chicago: Cowley Publications, 2004), 39–40.

19 Gordon Oyer, "Thomas Merton and the 'Pessimism' of Jacques Ellul," *Merton Annual: Studies in Culture, Spirituality and Social Concerns* 30 (2017): 131–44.

20 Merton, *Conjectures*, 70.

21 Anderson and Rainie, "The Future of Well-Being."

Chapter 1

Quoted in Noah Kulwin, "An Apology for the Internet—from the Architects Who Built It," *New York Magazine*, April 13, 2018, http://nymag.com/intelligencer/2018/04/an-apology-for-the -internet-from-the-people-who-built-it.html.

1   Richard Stokes, "I Left the Ad Industry Because Our Use of Data Tracking Terrified Me," *Fast Company*, June 6, 2019, https:// www.fastcompany.com/90359992/an-ad-tech-pioneer-on-where -our-data-economy-went-wrong-and-how-to-fix-it.

2   Simone Stolzoff, "Addicted to Your Smartphone? This Formula Is Why," *Wired*, February 1, 2018, https://www.wired.com/story/ phone-addiction-formula/.

3   Hilary Andersson, "Social Media Apps Are 'Deliberately' Addictive to Users," BBC, July 4, 2018, https://www.bbc.com/news/ technology-44640959.

4   Kulwin, "Apology for the Internet."

5   For a small sample of these trends, see Carole Cadwalladr, "My TED Talk: How I Took On the Tech Titans in Their Lair," *The Guardian*, April 21, 2019, https://www.theguardian.com/uk-news/ 2019/apr/21/carole-cadwalladr-ted-tech-google-facebook-zuckerberg -silicon-valley; and "How Tech Utopia Fostered Tyranny," *New Atlantis* 57 (Winter 2019): 3–13, https://www.thenewatlantis.com/ publications/how-tech-utopia-fostered-tyranny.

6   Nina Godlewski, "If You Have Over 25 Photos on Instagram, You're No Longer Cool," *Business Insider*, May 26, 2016, https:// www.businessinsider.com/teens-curate-their-instagram-accounts -2016-5.

7   Jean M. Twenge, "Have Smartphones Destroyed a Generation?" *The Atlantic*, September 2017, https://www.theatlantic.com/ magazine/archive/2017/09/has-the-smartphone-destroyed-a -generation/534198/.

8   Sherry Turkle, *Alone Together: Why We Expect Less from Each Other and More from Technology* (New York: Basic Books, 2011), 282.

9   Ibid., 284.

10 Bill Bryson, *The Life and Times of the Thunderbolt Kid: A Memoir* (New York: Broadway Books, 2006), 69–70.

11 Thomas Merton, *Conjectures of a Guilty Bystander* (New York: Image Books, 1965), 61.

12 Stolzoff, "Addicted to Your Smartphone?"

13 P. W. Singer and Emerson T. Brooking, *LikeWar: The Weaponization of Social Media* (New York: Houghton Mifflin Harcourt, 2018), 220, emphasis in the original. See also David Robson, "How the Color Red Warps the Mind," BBC, September 1, 2014, http://www.bbc.com/future/story/20140827-how-the-colour -red-warps-the-mind.

14 Merton, *Conjectures*, 71.

15 Yuval Noah Harari and Tristan Harris, "When Tech Knows You Better Than You Know Yourself," interview by Nicholas Thompson, *Wired*, October 4, 2018, https://www.wired.com/story/ artificial-intelligence-yuval-noah-harari-tristan-harris/.

16 Andersson, "Social Media Apps."

17 Paul Armstrong, "Facebook Is Helping Brands Target Teens Who Feel 'Worthless,'" *Forbes*, May 1, 2017, https://www.forbes .com/sites/paularmstrongtech/2017/05/01/facebook-is-helping -brands-target-teens-who-feel-worthless/.

18 Samuel Gibbs, "Facebook Apologises for Psychological Experiments on Users," *The Guardian*, July 2, 2014, https://www .theguardian.com/technology/2014/jul/02/facebook-apologises -psychological-experiments-on-users.

19 Tim Huebsch, "Matthew Inman of The Oatmeal Admits His Reason for Running: To Eat Cake," *Canadian Running Magazine*, November 11, 2015, https://runningmagazine.ca/video/matthew -inman-of-the-oatmeal-running/.

20 Robert Kozinets, "How Social Media Fires Peoples' Passions and Builds Extremist Divisions, *The Conversation*, November 13, 2017, http://theconversation.com/how-social-media-fires-peoples-passions -and-builds-extremist-divisions-86909.

21 See Sounman Hong, "Political Polarization on Twitter: Social

Media May Contribute to Online Extremism," Scholars at Harvard, accessed July 24, 2019, https://scholar.harvard.edu/sounman_hong/political-polarization-twitter-social-media-may-contribute-online-extremism.

22 Kozinets, "How Social Media Fires."

23 Ibid.

24 Kate Shellnut, "Russia's Fake Facebook Ads Targeted Christians," *Christianity Today*, November 3, 2017, https://www.christianitytoday.com/news/2017/november/russia-fake-facebook-election-ads-targeted-christian-voters.html.

25 Anita Wadhwani, "Mueller Report Outlines Activities of Fake Tennessee GOP Twitter Account Linked to Russians," *Tennessean*, April 18, 2019, https://www.tennessean.com/story/news/2019/04/18/mueller-report-release-shows-fake-tennessee-gop-twitter-account-link-russia/3507153002/.

26 Jason Parham, "Russians Posing as Black Activists on Facebook Is More Than Fake News," *Wired*, October 18, 2017, https://www.wired.com/story/russian-black-activist-facebook-accounts/.

27 Mike Glenn, "A Houston Protest, Organized by Russian Trolls," *Houston Chronicle*, February 20, 2018, https://www.houstonchronicle.com/local/gray-matters/article/A-Houston-protest-organized-by-Russian-trolls-12625481.php.

28 Caroline Haskins, "I Unknowingly Went to a Trump Protest Organized by Russian Agents," *Vice*, November 22, 2017, https://www.vice.com/en_us/article/ywb9kx/nyc-trump-election-protest-hack-russian-agents-trolls-government.

29 Chaim Gartenberg, "Seized Documents Reveal That Facebook Knew about Russian Data Harvesting as Early as 2014," *The Verge*, November 27, 2018, https://www.theverge.com/2018/11/27/18114228/facebook-russian-data-harvesting-documents-2014-uk-parliment-six4three.

30 Kulwin, "Apology for the Internet."

31 Thomas Merton, "The Christian in a Technological World," quoted in Phillip M. Thompson, *Returning to Reality: Thomas Merton's Wisdom for a Technological Age* (Cambridge, UK: Lutterworth Press, 2013), xiii.

Chapter 2

Thomas Merton, *Conjectures of a Guilty Bystander* (New York: Image Books, 1965), 113.

1 Ibid.

2 John Ortberg, "Ruthlessly Eliminate Hurry," *Christianity Today*, July 2002, https://www.christianitytoday.com/pastors/2002/july -online-only/cln20704.html.

3 Sherry Turkle, *Alone Together: Why We Expect Less from Each Other and More from Technology* (New York: Basic Books, 2011), 280.

4 Michele W. Berger, "Social Media Use Increases Depression and Loneliness," *Penn Today*, November 9, 2018, https://penntoday.upenn .edu/news/social-media-use-increases-depression-and-loneliness.

5 Bill Murphy Jr., "This Fascinating New Ivy League Study Shows the 'Clear Causal Link' between Facebook, Instagram and Snapchat and 'Loneliness and Depression,'" *INC*, November 23, 2018, https://www.inc.com/bill-murphy-jr/this-fascinating-new-ivy-league -study-shows-clear-causal-link-between-facebook-instagam-snapchat -loneliness-depression.html.

6 See "Is Social Media Making You Lonely?" *Psychology Today*, October 5, 2018, https://www.psychologytoday.com/us/blog/ modern-mentality/201810/is-social-media-making-you-lonely.

7 Shainna Ali, "What You Need to Know about the Loneliness Epidemic," *Psychology Today*, July 12, 2018, https://www .psychologytoday.com/us/blog/modern-mentality/201807/what -you-need-know-about-the-loneliness-epidemic.

8 Katherine Hobson, "Feeling Lonely? Too Much Time on Social Media May Be Why," NPR, March 6, 2017, https:// www.npr.org/sections/health-shots/2017/03/06/518362255/ feeling-lonely-too-much-time-on-social-media-may-be-why.

9 Tristan Harris, "Smartphone Addiction: The Slot Machine in Your Pocket," *Yale Global Online*, July 27, 2016, https://yaleglobal .yale.edu/content/smartphone-addiction-slot-machine-your-pocket.

10 Jon Ronson, "How One Stupid Tweet Blew Up Justine Sacco's Life," *New York Times*, February 12, 2015, https://www.nytimes .com/2015/02/15/magazine/how-one-stupid-tweet-ruined-justine -saccos-life.html.

11 Sean Aday, Deen Freelon, and Marc Lynch, "How Social Media

Undermined Egypt's Democratic Transition," *Washington Post*, October 7, 2016, https://www.washingtonpost.com/news/monkey -cage/wp/2016/10/07/how-social-media-undermined-egypts -democratic-transition/.

12 P. W. Singer and Emerson T. Brooking, *LikeWar: The Weaponization of Social Media* (New York: Houghton Mifflin Harcourt, 2018), 127.

13 Alex Hern, "'Never Get High on Your Own Supply'—Why Social Media Bosses Don't Use Social Media," January 23, 2018, *The Guardian*, https://www.theguardian.com/media/2018/jan/23/never -get-high-on-your-own-supply-why-social-media-bosses-dont-use -social-media.

14 Nick Bilton, "Steve Jobs Was a Low-Tech Parent," *New York Times*, September 10, 2014, https://www.nytimes.com/2014/09/11/ fashion/steve-jobs-apple-was-a-low-tech-parent.html.

15 Komal Nathani, "The Techpreneurs of Silicon Valley Are Keeping Their Families Away from Technology. Should You Too?" *Entrepreneur*, August 30, 2018, https://www.entrepreneur.com/ article/319288.

16 Hern, "'Never Get High.'"

17 Jean M. Twenge, "Have Smartphones Destroyed a Generation?" *The Atlantic*, September 2017, https://www.theatlantic.com/ magazine/archive/2017/09/has-the-smartphone-destroyed-a -generation/534198/.

18 Chris Weller, "Bill Gates and Steve Jobs Raised Their Kids Tech-Free—and It Should've Been a Red Flag," *The Independent*, October 24, 2017, https://www.independent.co.uk/life-style/ gadgets-and-tech/bill-gates-and-steve-jobs-raised-their-kids-techfree -and-it-shouldve-been-a-red-flag-a8017136.html.

19 Bella DePaulo, "What's Trump Doing in Your Therapy Room?" *Psychology Today*, June 7, 2018, https://www.psychologytoday.com/ us/blog/living-single/201806/what-s-trump-doing-in-your-therapy -room.

20 "APA *Stress in America* Survey: US at 'Lowest Point We Can Remember;' Future of Nation Most Commonly Reported Source of Stress," *American Psychological Association*, November 1, 2017, https://www.apa.org/news/press/releases/2017/11/lowest-point.

21 Bharat N. Anand, "The U.S. Media's Problems Are Much Bigger

Than Fake News and Filter Bubbles," *Harvard Business Review*, January 5, 2017, https://hbr.org/2017/01/the-u-s-medias-problems -are-much-bigger-than-fake-news-and-filter-bubbles.

22 "APA *Stress in America* Survey."

23 Elisa Shearer, "Social Media Outpaces Print Newspapers in the U.S. as a News Source," Pew Research Center, December 10, 2018, https://www.pewresearch.org/fact-tank/2018/12/10/social-media -outpaces-print-newspapers-in-the-u-s-as-a-news-source/.

24 Robinson Meyer, "The Grim Conclusions of the Largest-Ever Study of Fake News," *The Atlantic*, March 8, 2018, https://www .theatlantic.com/technology/archive/2018/03/largest-study-ever-fake -news-mit-twitter/555104/.

25 Stefan Wojcik, Solomon Messing, Aaron Smith, Lee Rainie, and Paul Hitlin, "Bots in the Twittersphere," Pew Research Center, April 9, 2018, https://www.pewinternet.org/2018/04/09/ bots-in-the-twittersphere/.

26 Michael Newberg, "As Many as 48 Million Twitter Accounts Aren't People, Says Study," CNBC, March 10, 2017, https://www .cnbc.com/2017/03/10/nearly-48-million-twitter-accounts-could-be -bots-says-study.html. See also Selina Wang, "Twitter Is Crawling with Bots and Lacks Incentive to Expel Them," Bloomberg, October 13, 2017, https://www.bloomberg.com/news/articles/2017-10-13/ twitter-is-crawling-with-bots-and-lacks-incentive-to-expel-them; and Selina Wang, "Twitter Sidestepped Russian Account Warnings, Former Worker Says," Bloomberg, November 3, 2017, https://www .bloomberg.com/news/articles/2017-11-03/former-twitter-employee -says-fake-russian-accounts-were-not-taken-seriously.

27 Merton, *Conjectures*, 59.

28 Singer and Brooking, *LikeWar*, 154.

29 Ibid., 158.

30 Jaron Lanier, "Global Addiction to Social Media Is Ruining Democracy," *Boston Globe*, June 8, 2018, https://www.bostonglobe .com/opinion/2018/06/07/global-addiction-social-media-ruining -democracy/Ta9316Ma628HQaJ5PyM8uI/story.html.

31 Daniella Balarezo and Daryl Chen, "How to Read the News Like a Scientist," Ideas TED, March 22, 2019, https://ideas.ted.com/ how-to-read-the-news-like-a-scientist/.

32 Peter Dizikes, "Study: On Twitter, false news travels faster than

true stories," MIT News, March 8, 2018, http://news.mit.edu/2018/
study-twitter-false-news-travels-faster-true-stories-0308.

33 Craig Timberg, "Russian Propaganda Effort Helped Spread 'Fake
News' During Election, Experts Say," *Washington Post*, November 24,
2016, https://www.washingtonpost.com/business/economy/russian
-propaganda-effort-helped-spread-fake-news-during-election-experts
-say/2016/11/24/793903b6-8a40-4ca9-b712-716af66098fe_story
.html; Colleen Shalby, "Facts about Fake News's Influence on U.S.
Elections and the Fight against Misinformation," *L.A. Times*,
March 19, 2019, https://www.latimes.com/science/la-sci-sn-fake
-news-election-20190319-story.html; Alexander Smith and Vladimir
Banic, "Fake News: How a Partying Macedonian Teen Earns
Thousands Publishing Lies," NBC, December 9, 2016, https://www
.nbcnews.com/news/world/fake-news-how-partying-macedonian
-teen-earns-thousands-publishing-lies-n692451.

34 Singer and Brooking, *LikeWar*, 131.

35 Camila Domonoske, "Students Have 'Dismaying' Inability to
Tell Fake News from Real, Study Finds," NPR, November 23, 2016,
https://www.npr.org/sections/thetwo-way/2016/11/23/503129818/
study-finds-students-have-dismaying-inability-to-tell-fake-news
-from-real.

36 Merton, *Conjectures*, 96.

37 Samanth Subramanian, "The Macedonian Teens Who Mastered
Fake News," *Wired*, February 15, 2017, https://www.wired.com/
2017/02/veles-macedonia-fake-news/.

38 Merton, *Conjectures*, 72

39 Jacques Ellul, "New Hope for the Technological Society: An
Interview with Jacques Ellul," interview by Berta Sichel, *ETC: A
Review of General Semantics* 40, no. 2 (July 1, 1983): 202.

40 Christopher Hebert, "My Year of Living Ignorantly: I Entered
a News Blackout the Day Trump Was Elected," *The Guardian*,
January 18, 2018, https://www.theguardian.com/lifeandstyle/2018/
jan/18/my-year-of-living-ignorantly-i-entered-a-news-blackout-the
-day-trump-was-elected.

Chapter 3

Thomas Merton, "Letter to Rachel Carson," *Witness to Freedom*,
quoted in Maria Popova, "Technology, Wisdom, and the Difficult

Art of Civilizational Self-Awareness: Thomas Merton's Beautiful Letter of Appreciation to Rachel Carson for Catalyzing the Environmental Movement," *Brain Pickings*, November 14, 2017, https://www.brainpickings.org/2017/11/14/thomas-merton-rachel-carson-letter/.

1   Henri J. M. Nouwen, *The Way of the Heart: Connecting with God through Prayer, Wisdom, and Silence* (New York: Seabury, 1981), 19–21.

2   Sherry Turkle, *Alone Together: Why We Expect Less from Each Other and More from Technology* (New York: Basic Books, 2011), 185.

3   Ibid., 280.

4   Taylor Lorenz, "Teens Are Being Bullied 'Constantly' on Instagram: Harassment on the Platform Can Be Uniquely Cruel, and for Many It Feels like There's No Escape," *The Atlantic*, October 10, 2018, https://www.theatlantic.com/technology/archive/2018/10/teens-face-relentless-bullying-instagram/572164/.

5   Thomas Merton, *No Man Is an Island* (New York: Mariner Books, 2002), 178.

6   Ibid., 127.

7   Martin Laird, *An Ocean of Light: Contemplation, Transformation, and Liberation* (New York: Oxford University Press, 2019), 119.

8   Ibid., 62.

9   See Thomas Keating, *Open Mind, Open Heart* (New York: Continuum, 2008), 19–23.

10 Thomas Merton, *Thoughts in Solitude* (New York: Farrar, Straus and Giroux, 1999), 2.

11 Colman McCarthy, "When Thomas Merton Called Me 'Utterly Stupid,'" *National Catholic Reporter*, December 17, 2018, https://www.ncronline.org/news/opinion/when-thomas-merton-called-me-utterly-stupid.

12 Adam Altar, *Irresistible: The Rise of Addictive Technology and the Business of Keeping Us Hooked* (New York: Penguin, 2017), 238–39.

13 Ibid., 228–29.

Chapter 4

Henri J. M. Nouwen, *The Way of the Heart: Connecting with God through Prayer, Wisdom, and Silence* (New York: Seabury, 1981), 25–26.

1   Bob Smietana, "Most Churches Offer Wi-Fi but Skip Twitter,"

LifeWay Research, January 9, 2018, https://lifewayresearch.com/
2018/01/09/most-churches-offer-free-wi-fi-but-skip-twitter/.

2   "State of the Bible 2017: Top Findings," Barna Group, accessed
June 18, 2019, https://www.barna.com/research/state-bible-2017
-top-findings/.

3   Jeff Brumley, "Churches Must Count the Cost of Pursuing
Youth on Social Media," *Baptist News Global*, June 19, 2018, https://
baptistnews.com/article/churches-must-count-the-cost-of-pursuing
-youth-on-social-media/.

4   Rich Burch, "3 Reasons Your Church Shouldn't Be Running
Facebook Ads This Easter," *unSeminary*, April 19, 2019, https://
unseminary.com/3-reasons-your-church-shouldnt-be-running
-facebook-ads-this-easter/.

5   Lauren Cassani Davis, "The Flight from Conversation" *The
Atlantic*, October 7, 2015, https://www.theatlantic.com/technology/
archive/2015/10/reclaiming-conversation-sherry-turkle/409273/.

6   Howard Thurman, *Essential Writings* (New York: Orbis Books,
2006), 57.

Chapter 5

Thomas Merton, *Conjectures of a Guilty Bystander* (New York: Image
Books, 1965), 155–56.

1   Ibid., 153–55

2   Howard Thurman, *Essential Writings* (New York: Orbis Books,
2006), 48–49.

3   Thomas Merton, *Contemplative Prayer* (New York: Image Books,
1969), 46–47.

4   Ibid., 49.

5   Henri J. M. Nouwen, *The Way of the Heart: Connecting with God
through Prayer, Wisdom, and Silence* (New York: Seabury, 1981), 26.

6   Ibid., 26, 28.

7   Merton, *Contemplative Prayer*, 47.

8   Martin Laird, *An Ocean of Light: Contemplation, Transformation,
and Liberation* (New York: Oxford University Press, 2019), 58.

9   Thurman, *Essential Writings*, 45.

10   Laird, *An Ocean of Light*, 66.

11   Thomas Keating, *Open Mind, Open Heart* (New York:
Continuum, 2008), 27–28.

12 Laird, *An Ocean of Light*, 5.

13 Ibid., 67.

14 Ibid., 13.

15 Thomas Merton, *The Seven Storey Mountain* (New York: Harcourt, 1999), 356.

16 Nouwen, *The Way of the Heart*, 37.

17 Laird, *An Ocean of Light*, 100.

18 David Rakoff, "Steven Seagal: I Can't Believe It's Not Buddha," *GQ*, August 9, 2012, https://www.gq.com/story/steven-seagal -buddhism-david-rakoff.

19 Merton, *Contemplative Prayer*, 50.

20 Ibid., 47, emphasis in the original.

21 Quoted in Laird, *An Ocean of Light*, 12.

Chapter 6

Story of a Soul: The Autobiography of Saint Thérèse of Lisieux, 3rd ed., trans. John Clarke (Washington, DC: ICS Publications, 1996), 151.

1   Richard J. Foster, *Casting a Vision: The Past and Future of Spiritual Formation* (Denver: Renovaré, 2019), 9.

2   Michele W. Berger, "Social Media Use Increases Depression and Loneliness," *Penn Today*, November 9, 2018, https://penntoday .upenn.edu/news/social-media-use-increases-depression-and -loneliness. See also Jeremy Nobel, "Does Social Media Make You Lonely?," *Harvard Health Publishing*, December 21, 2018, https:// www.health.harvard.edu/blog/is-a-steady-diet-of-social-media -unhealthy-2018122115600.

3   Howard Thurman, *Essential Writings* (New York: Orbis Books, 2006), 60–61.

4   Thomas Merton, *Contemplative Prayer* (New York: Image Books, 1969), 47, 48.

5   Ibid., 45.

6   Thurman, *Essential Writings*, 46.

7   Quoted in Martin Laird, *Into the Silent Land: A Guide to the Christian Practice of Contemplation* (New York: Oxford University Press, 2006), 51.

8   Martin Laird, *An Ocean of Light: Contemplation, Transformation, and Liberation* (New York: Oxford University Press, 2019), 98.

9   Ibid., 67.

10 Ibid., 97.

11 Thurman, *Essential Writings*, 60.

12 Quoted in Merton, *Contemplative Prayer*, 5.

13 Thomas Merton, *The Inner Experience: Notes on Contemplation* (New York: HarperCollins, 2003), 152–53.

Chapter 7

Howard Thurman, *Essential Writings* (New York: Orbis Books, 2006), 61.

1   Jessica Greif and Melissa Binder, "What Life Is Like as a Modern-Day Monk," *The Oregonian*, July 28, 2015, video, 4:28, https://www.youtube.com/watch?v=sF7-vN_qCF4.

2   Sr. Carly Paula Arcella as told to Catie L'Heureux, "What It's Like to Be a Young Nun," *The Cut*, March 8, 2018, https://www.thecut.com/2018/03/what-its-like-to-be-a-young-nun.html.

3   Penelope Green, "Bucking a Trend: Some Millennials Are Seeking a Nun's Life," *New York Times*, September 5, 2018, https://www.nytimes.com/2015/09/06/fashion/dominican-nuns-of-summit-a-nuns-life.html.

4   See Kristen Weir, "The Power of Self-Control," *Monitor on Psychology* 43, no. 1 (January 2012): 36, https://www.apa.org/monitor/2012/01/self-control.

5   Henri J. M. Nouwen, *The Way of the Heart: Connecting with God through Prayer, Wisdom, and Silence* (New York: Seabury, 1981), 30.

6   Thomas Merton, *Wisdom of the Desert* (New York: New Directions, 1960), 23.

Chapter 8

Madeline L'Engle, *The Rock That Is Higher: Story as Truth* (Colorado Springs: WaterBrook Press, 1993), 220.

1   See Randy A. Sansone, and Lori A. Sansone, "Gratitude and Well-Being," *Psychiatry* 7, no. 11 (November 2010): 18–22, https://www.ncbi.nlm.nih.gov/pmc/articles/PMC3010965/.

2   Jacques Ellul, "New Hope for the Technological Society: An Interview with Jacques Ellul," interview by Berta Sichel, *ETC: A Review of General Semantics* 40, no. 2 (July 1, 1983): 196.

3   Jacques Launay, "Choir Singing Improves Health, Happiness, and Is the Perfect Icebreaker," University of Oxford, accessed June

12, 2019, http://www.ox.ac.uk/research/choir-singing-improves
-health-happiness-%E2%80%93-and-perfect-icebreaker.

4   Stacy Horn, "Research Shows Singing in a Choir Increases
Happiness," *Slate*, July 25, 2013, https://slate.com/human-interest/
2013/07/singing-in-a-choir-research-shows-it-increases-happiness
.html.

5   Philip M. Thompson, *Returning to Reality: Thomas Merton's
Wisdom for a Technological Age* (Cambridge, UK: Lutterworth Press,
2013), 86.

THE AUTHOR

ED CYZEWSKI is the author of *Flee, Be Silent, Pray: Ancient Prayers for Anxious Christians*; *A Christian Survival Guide*; and other books. His writing has appeared in *Christianity Today* and *Leadership Journal*, and he blogs at *This Kinda Contemplative Life* on Patheos. Cyzewski leads contemplative prayer retreats, including the Renew and Refine Retreat for writers. Cyzewski has a master of divinity from Biblical Theological Seminary in Philadelphia and works as a freelance writer and editor. He and his wife have three children. Connect with him at www.EdCyzewski.com.